DAVENPORT'S FLORIDA WILLS AND ESTATE PLANNING LEGAL FORMS

DAVENPORT'S FLORIDA WILLS AND ESTATE PLANNING LEGAL FORMS

NEW EDITION

written by attorneys
Alex Russell and Robert Maxwell

Published by Davenport Publishing

PUBLICATION DATA

(informal, library may use different data)

Names: Russell, Alex, 1972- author ; Maxwell, Robert, 1960- author

Title: Davenport's Florida Wills And Estate Planning Legal Forms

Other Titles: Davenport's Wills

Description: Davenport Publishing 2022

Suggested Other Identifiers: 9798363995767, LCCN 2021909030, 9798748423373

Subjects: LCSH: Wills--United States;
                Wills--United States--Forms;
                Estate Planning--United States;
                Legal Forms

Classification: LFF KF755 .C55 2022 (or as library chooses)
                DDC 346.73 Rus--dc23 (or as library chooses)

WARNING

PERMISSION TO COPY AND USE BOOKS FOR FREE

BOOKS AND FORMS FOR OTHER STATES ARE AVAILABLE

Alabama	Hawaii	Missouri	Pennsylvania
Alaska	Idaho	Nebraska	Rhode Island
Arizona	Indiana	Nevada	South Carolina
Arkansas	Iowa	New Jersey	South Dakota
California	Kansas	New Mexico	Tennessee
Colorado	Kentucky	New York	Texas
Connecticut	Maryland	Ohio	Vermont
Delaware	Minnesota	Oklahoma	
Georgia	Mississippi	Oregon	

TABLE OF CONTENTS

CHAPTER 1
BOOK BASICS AND LIST OF FORMS

"ESTATE PLANNING" CONTROLS THINGS IF LATER ABSENT, SICK, OR DEAD

From Davenport Publishing and written by attorneys this book covers "Estate Planning" which is doing legal documents to later control health care, property, money, children, and funeral if absent, sick, or dead.

FLORIDA LAW APPLIES TO MOST PEOPLE HERE OR PLANNING TO RETURN

This book is for Florida state and forms for 1 state cannot be safely used elsewhere. State law in this legal area applies if a person: a) resides here as a main home, or b) resided here and left with firm plans to return even if living in a home elsewhere years like some students, military, and some workers on projects. For health care people should consider doing forms to match state of hospital or facility they may use.

SHORT BOOK WITH FORMS USES TITLES, EMPHASIS, AND BLANK PAGES

This book written by attorneys is short so may read rough but lets person read in day basics of this area. The book also has ready-to-use legal forms people can quickly see. For emphasis paragraph titles, boxes, and underling of parts is used. To save room some small words are skipped and quote marks put before periods (the older way). Some legal words are capitalized like Will, Testator, and Agent but this is optional. Back side of pages are blank which is optional but common for legal forms and makes photocopying easy

PEOPLE CAN IN A FEW WAYS GET FORMS, FILL IN SOME BLANKS, THEN SIGN

To get forms people can 1) photocopy pages from book (available places like Amazon.com), 2) tear or cut out pages from book, or 3) at www.davenportpublishing.com download PDF or Word Doc of book with forms. Forms should have page numbers whited-out, and if doing forms confirm no page numbers appear at bottom. To fill in forms use computer or handwrite using pen, marker, or even pencil. Many spaces may be left blank. When no more changes will be made people should sign and date in ink (with witnesses or notary if needed). Most forms use blank spaces and underlining to show where to add words (like, "I give _____ to _____").

FORMS ARE BINDING LEGAL DOCUMENTS AND USUALLY WORK WELL

Legal forms make binding legal documents that judges, doctors, families, banks, and others must follow. Instead of forms a lawyer can be paid to write documents but may cost $2,000+ per person, take months of meetings, push complex options, give or receive incorrect information, make mistakes, charge to re-do forms every few years, and often a lawyer is not an Estate Planning expert and just uses legal forms too. In life people weigh costs and benefits and often pick a low cost option despite risk. Estate Planning studies show a surprising 60% of people die without doing anything, 19% use a lawyer, and 21% use legal forms.

ESTATE PLANNING DOES SIMPLE THINGS WITH PERSON SAYING WHAT TO DO

Estate Planning does mostly simple things that forms are good at, like saying who gets things, who does a job, and health care agent and wishes. Estate Planning even if done sloppily usually works fine. A person has a legal right to control their health care, property, and family issues, and judges, doctors, or others basically ask: **"Based on what person wrote what did they likely want done?"**

BOOK AND FORMS SUIT PEOPLE WITHOUT STRANGE SITUATIONS OR WISHES

This book and forms can't cover everything but should suit people without strange situations or wishes about Estate Planning, which is probably over 80% of people. Most people know if they have strange wishes or situations in this area so are in the small fraction who maybe should do legal research or see a lawyer. Strange situations or wishes that may call for research or lawyer include: a) wish to make unusual gifts of property and money, b) wish for things to go to person with "special needs", c) wish to hide assets to qualify for government programs, d) big family medical concerns like extreme age, or e) wealth over $3 million.

BOOK COVERS LAW MOST PEOPLE NEED AND SOME STATE DIFFERENCES

This book covers what most people want to know. State laws across the USA are mostly similar and this book covers the normal law, and this book also covers some ways Florida state law is different. People in some cases may want to research Florida state law further or go see a lawyer.

BOOK PROVIDES FLORIDA "STANDARD FORM" OR SUITABLE FORM

Often a Florida agency, hospital, or the legislature has made a form most people in state use and call the "standard form", and doctors, judges, or others may not like a different form. This book does provide the standard form in a legal area if it exists, and in other areas the authors have written a suitable form. Making small changes to forms is rare but often fine if what is wanted is clear.

COSTLY ESTATE PLANNING OFTEN IS LESS GOOD THAN LIFE INSURANCE

Estate Planning is not worth as much effort and money as people think, especially if using costly lawyer and not legal forms. It often does not: create new wealth, cut taxes except for multi-millionaires, cut most later costs or delays, or affect health care unless person is suddenly incapacitated and rush decision needed. For young adults or parents the benefit of costly Estate Planning seems low since only about 8.8% of people die before 60, and only 0.2% of children under 19 had 2 parents die to probably really need a guardian. *See Social Security Census Tables by Felicitie Bell; Life Factors & Mortality Study (Census Study 288).* So advice that people pay $2,000+ repeatedly in life for complex Estate Planning seems bad. Instead of doing this just saving money can help family, or people can buy term life insurance via questionnaire without an exam ("simplified issue") of $80,000 for $40+ monthly or $400+ yearly from MetLife, Haven, SBLI, or AIG.

OTHER FORMS NOT IN THIS BOOK ARE LESS HELPFUL AND LESS COMMON

This book skips providing some less useful documents.

A person may do papers for "Revocable Living Trust" so Trust holds during their life all money and things. This may after death avoid small delay, costs, and work (by "avoiding probate"). Few do this as it means the hassle of moving all person has into Trust for years all for small benefits for others who are happy to inherit.

A "Codicil" can modify Will but it's best to just re-do Will.

A person may add to Will some "Childrens Trust" "papers so Trust will hold minor child's property or money until 18, but this is rare since this can be costly hassle, children rarely get much of value, and options exist like a Will naming or judge naming a "guardian" to manage and decide how to spend things for child.

Some do "Pet Trust" to arrange money for pet, but it is easy to give both pet and money to friend in Will.

Separate "Organ Donation" forms exist but most do this in other form or in Drivers License or State ID.

ESTATE PLANNING DOES SIMPLE THINGS IN 3 MAIN AREAS WITH 10 FORMS

Estate Planning seems complex but mostly is a person doing documents to control their life in 3 areas: a) After Death , b) Health Care , and c) Giving Power . Forms can overlap or duplicate each other a lot. Most people do 1 or 2 forms like many people do 1 Will and 1 health care form, but some people do more. Many people re-do forms every 10 years or so. This book covers 10 Florida legal documents (see below).

AFTER DEATH FORMS

Form 1. Last Will And Testament (Standard) – lets person control some things after death especially gifts of property and money, and this Form 1 is the most used Will in this book and suits most people.

Form 2. Last Will And Testament (Guardians) – this is Will with parts added to name a "Guardian" or similar to if needed care for minor child under 18, and also person to care for their estate and property.

Form 3. Self-Proving Affidavit – done with Will to help later work of showing Will was properly signed.

Form 4. Tangible Personal Property List – lets person easily after Will is done write more gifts to occur after death of "tangible personal property" like cars, furniture, jewelry, tools, and clothes.

HEALTH CARE FORMS

Form 5. Designation Of Health Care Surrogate – this is often the only health care form done and it lets person be named "Surrogate" to if needed control health care and lets health care instructions be written.

Form 6. Living Will – this form does extreme act of in writing refusing most further health care **if later** doctors think a person's health situation has gotten very bad and more care likely won't help.

Form 7. Do Not Resuscitate Order – does extreme act of saying **immediately from now on** do not give certain health care (mainly C.P.R.), and says this in 1 page form to be read fast outside a facility (and this book also has the P.O.L.S.T. form with more options about care to not give).

GIVING POWER FORMS

Form 8. Durable Power Of Attorney – lets power over money, property, and more be shared during life with "Agent" or "Attorney-in-Fact" who often is spouse, adult child, or friend so they can help do things.

Form 9. Designation Of Health Care Surrogate Of Minor – lets parent share power over health care of child under 18 with person like relative or friend watching child to let them quickly make decisions if needed.

Form 10. Inter Vivos Authorization of Legally Authorized Person – lets instructions be written and person named to control funeral and bodily remains instead of following law saying closest family does this.

CHAPTER 2
TERMS, PROPERTY, AND HELPFUL INFORMATION FORM

THERE ARE BASIC TERMS AND IDEAS IN WILLS AND ESTATE PLANNING

Some legal terms and ideas are basic to Wills and Estate Planning.

■ "Estate Planning" is a person doing legal documents to control things if later they are absent, sick, or dead. After form is signed person is still free to sell or transfer property, instruct doctors, or change forms.

■ A person who has died is called "decedent" or "deceased". People getting gifts like by Will can be called "beneficiary" or "heir" if related (they "inherit"). "Survive" or "surviving" means to be alive after someone dies.

■ A "Will" or "will" (this book uses upper case "W") is legal document done to control issues after death. The phrase "Last Will And Testament" is used since "Testament" long ago was a separate document done with a Will to do similar things. If no Will is done it is called being "in testate". A person doing Will is called "Testator" or "Will maker". A female Testator use to be called "Testatrix" and female Executor an "Executrix".

■ "Residue Clause" put at end of Will gifts property or money left over to persons named in the clause.

■ "Probate" is legal process to do things after death like transfer property, pick guardian, and pay creditors. Due to nice recent changes probate is now often "informal", faster, and less expensive.

■ A "Personal Representative" is person usually named in a Will to do things after someone's death like probate and transfer property. "Executor" is the old term for this and this book mostly still uses this word.

■ "Guardian of the Person" cares for child under 18 if needed. "Guardian of the Property" manages and says how to spend child's money and property on them (called "Guardian of the Estate" in other states).

■ "Notary" (also called "notary public") is a person approved by a state to see signings and stamp forms, and is found in banks, courts, insurance agents, or often a phonebook. Certain forms must be notarized.

■ "Agent" (also written "agent" with lower case letter) is title often used for person that works for someone.

■ "Property" is either: 1) "real property" which is land and buildings ("real estate"), 2) "personal property" which is things not real property, like cash, accounts, stocks, investments, tools, clothes, cars, jewelry, art, or 3) "fixtures" which are things tied to real property (like fences, posts, lighting, and wired-in appliances).

■ A "Power of Attorney" document is done by person (called "Principal") to give power to someone (called "Agent" or "Attorney-in-Fact") to do things, but person giving power keeps power, so power is really shared.

■ Forms to control health care are often called "Health Care Directives", but names vary.

■ State law is the "Florida Statutes" made up of "sections" often called statutes, shown by "§" or "s", and a reference to a law looks like, "Fla.Stat. § 403.11". Wills and similar are handled by the "Circuit Court" and "Probate" office. A form put in statues by legislature for people to find and use if wanted is a "statutory form".

MAYBE DO NEW DOCUMENTS IF DIVORCE, MARRY, HAVE CHILD, OR MOVE

Divorcing, marrying, having a new child, or moving to a new state can have big legal effects, and if any of these events occur it is recommended people do a new Will and other Estate Planning papers soon. To help, most states say Will from another state is still valid, and say divorce cancels Will gifts to ex-spouse.

"INTESTATE" LAW SAYS WHERE THINGS GO AT DEATH IF THERE IS NO WILL

State "intestate law" says where property and money goes if no valid Will was done before person died (except for certain rights of spouses, family, and creditors). Intestacy laws often say half and sometimes all goes to surviving spouse if any, then half or any remainder goes to decedent's children (or if dead their own child gets that share), then all distant family, and then the state. Many people are happy with intestate law and intentionally die with no Will. For intestate law an adopted child counts but not foster-child or step-child.

"ESTATE" MEANS PROPERTY OF DECEDENT OR ENTITY HOLDING THINGS

The "Estate" or "probate estate" is all property and money of a person that on death did not somehow automatically transfer to other owners. "Estate" is also the word for a temporary entity run by Executor to do things after a death (sort of like a small corporation). A dead person's money and accounts might be renamed or moved to a bank account under an Estate name, like "Estate of John Eric Smith".

"PROBATE" IS LEGAL PROCESS USED AFTER A DEATH AND OFTEN IS EASY

"Probate" is legal process to do things after death. Due to nice legal changes probate is now often "informal" and faster and cheap. A standard case often is just filing page to open case, judge's order people obey Executor, contacting banks or similar to say money and property is controlled by Executor, transferring things to new owners, handling creditors of deceased, and filing a few pages to tell judge what was done.

WARNING: "NON-PROBATE PROPERTY" TRANSFERS IGNORE ANY WILL

Money or property that for some reason automatically transfers on death to other owners is called "non-probate property", and such things quickly transfer as arranged even if a Will names the same items. Examples are: a) "designated beneficiary" form done earlier names person to get accounts or investments, b) transfer-on-death account, c) real estate like house held by 2 people as "joint tenants with survivorship" or similar so survivor gets things. Property and money already in a Trust also ignores a Will and transfers as the trust papers say. Insurance usually ignores a Will and goes to the named beneficiary.

Trying to do non-probate transfers for all things is "avoiding probate", but it is rare as it may make living and paperwork a hassle for years, benefits are small, and often a thing is missed so probate will be done. When doing a Will a person should consider non-probate transfers that will occur automatically on death and consider what property and money will be left to transfer by Will.

PERSON CAN ONLY GIFT IN WILL WHAT THEY OWN AT DEATH

A person can only gift by Will things they own at death so people should research what they own.

Basically by law a person usually owns all they earn as wages and salary, owns their share of income and profit tied to property they own, and owns or partly owns things their money buys or improves. But married people in Community Property law states may face different rules.

For property with "title" documents (real estate or vehicles) or where there is a "listed owner" (like accounts) the named persons are usually the legal owners unless evidence shows special circumstances.

Note, a person during life can sell property, make gifts, or transfer things even if items are named in a Will, so people should consider if they already sold or gave away property they also name in a Will gift.

THINGS OWNED IN SPECIAL WAYS MAY LIMIT WILL GIFTING

A person should consider if they own real estate or other property in special ways which may limit gifting by Will. Laws vary but some special joint ways are:

    a) "joint tenant with right of survivorship" or similar so then property transfers automatically to the other named owners regardless of a Will, which in some states is often how a family house is held,

    b) a "life estate" so then other people named in paperwork get things at a death,

    c) "trust property" if paperwork made a trust and property was actually transferred to it, so then the trust papers and any trustee person control where things put in the trust go on someone's death.

But normal joint property for the part owned often can be gifted by Will, like "I give half of Boat that I own with Aunt Jo to Ed Fox". Joint ownership can occur if people do joint papers, agree to own jointly, buy with joint funds, a gift is to multiple persons, or if married and in a Community Law state something is bought.

USUALLY NO FEDERAL OR FLORIDA TAX IS OWED DUE TO A DEATH

Usually no tax is owed due to a death, including no estate, inheritance, death, or similar taxes. This is because the "Federal Estate And Gift Tax" only starts when tax credit is used up that covers $12.06 million per person in 2022 (with yearly rises for inflation). The state of Florida and all its counties and cities no longer have an estate tax, inheritance tax, or similar tax triggered or owed upon death. A few states have estate or inheritance taxes for things there going to people outside their state, but often they have a credit exempting the first $3 million in value so this rarely is a problem to outsiders. So, usually only multi-millionaires need to worry about estate or inheritance taxes in Florida.

SOME PEOPLE DO "HELPFUL INFORMATION" FORM (SEE ON NEXT PAGE)

It is not a real legal form that legally does anything but a person can do a "Helpful Information" form so family or friends after person's death have more information about property, money, locations, wishes, debts, documents, passwords, tips, and more. Neatness is not needed and often person does a quick draft, and later adds more details maybe on further pages, and maybe prints screenshots of account info to attach. Often people do most gifting using a Residue Clause in Will saying anything leftover goes to person named in the clause, so doing a Helpful Information form lets family know what property and money to look for. This form is often kept with a Will to at death go to Executor or family. See 2 page form on next pages.

ESTATE PLANNING HELPFUL INFORMATION

For more space attach copies of form or blank pages. Keep pages by Will or other place for Executor or family.

1. Personal Information (Name, Birthdate, Social Security #, special family details, other):

2. Real estate, vehicles, and other tangible property of high value (especially if people may not find them):

3. Non-tangible assets like stocks, accounts, investments, loans owed you, and businesses of high value:

4. Possible income or insurance of high value like pensions, retirement, disability, insurance, or contracts:

5. Debts owed by you like credit card, loan, student loan, mortgage, vehicle loan, and accounts payable:

6. Names and contact information of professionals used (attorneys, accountants, brokers, doctors, others):

7. Computer passwords and helpful files, document places, and safes or safe-deposit boxes codes/keys:

8. Other helpful things, wishes for funeral, special requests, and any last messages to family and friends:

CHAPTER 3
WILL BASICS

WILL LETS "TESTATOR" CONTROL SOME THINGS AFTER THEIR DEATH

Will is legal document done by person to control some things after death, like who gets person's money and property, who is Executor, who is Guardian for child, and say to use easier legal options. To do a Will a person must be at least age 18 and <u>when signing</u> be of sound mind (rational with sufficient memory) and not under duress (illegal pressure or threat). Verbal promises or even some writings about things to occur after death are usually invalid outside a proper Will. Person doing a Will for themselves is called the "Will maker" or more often the "Testator" (and "Testatrix" used to be used for women Testators).

WILL MUST BE IN WRITING AND SIGNED WITH 2 WITNESSES

To be valid a Will must show it is meant as a Will, and usually person must sign in front of 2 witnesses who sign too. Some people initial each Will page but this is not required. A few states let any ship crew, military, or people near death do Oral Will that is temporarily, but this is rare and risky and not covered here. Some states but not Florida let people skip 2 witnesses if a Will is all handwritten. Florida if special things are done now allows certain electronic signing of Wills, but this is new and rare and not covered in this book. Despite what is often seen on TV usually a "Video Will" or "Audio Will" not in writing has no power.

WITNESS MUST BE AT LEAST 18 AND PREFERABLY NOT NAMED IN WILL

<u>The 2 witnesses to a Will signing can be anyone at least age 18</u> but preferably not old or living far away. Florida law says people getting Will gifts <u>can</u> be witnesses and Will gifts to them are valid, but using these people may seem suspicious to judge or family and is best avoided if not a hassle (so lawyers prefer to use "disinterested witnesses"). State law also <u>does</u> let person named Executor or Guardian in Will be a witness but lawyers try to avoid this too. Often witness is friend, employee somewhere, stranger, spouse, or family.

TESTATOR AND 2 WITNESSES WHEN TOGETHER SIGN WILL

To do Will a Testator signs, then 2 witnesses usually sign in minutes. Witnesses just read the paragraph they sign and not the whole Will. Everyone should be in 1 room and see hand of each person as they sign. Technically a Testator can sign Will alone and later just "acknowledge" signature to witnesses who then sign, but few do this. Witnesses showing ID is not required but usual. A Testator need not use their full legal name if they dislike it. Testator initialing each Will page is not required. It is not required but some Testators chat 5 minutes to witnesses to show they're of sound mind and not being forced. It is not required in Florida but some Testators tell witnesses "This is my Will" and hold it up (some states call this "publishing" a Will).

KEEP SIGNED WILL IN SAFE PLACE IT CAN BE FOUND FAST AFTER DEATH

People should keep Will so it can found within days of death, like in desk, drawer, safe, or less often safe deposit box. Or it can be given to someone to hold. It may help to tell someone where to find Will and a key. Unlike some states Wills usually won't be accepted by a Florida Court during Testator's life for safekeeping.

CANCELLING OLD WILLS IS USUALLY NOT A PROBLEM

So a new Will is followed old Wills should be canceled ("revoked") but this is easy. A person can say old

Wills are revoked in new Will and most do this, write "void" or "cancelled" or big X on old Will, or just rip up or trash old Will. But crossing out parts of a Will has no effect, and revoking Will doesn't bring back earlier Wills.

MOST WILLS SAY USE LESS COSTLY AND SHORTER "INFORMAL" PROBATE

Usually the probate process is not too slow or costly. To help most Wills say "use informal probate" which skips some hearings, filings, and other things. Usually well over 95% of value does get to recipients.

"PERSONAL REPRESENTATIVE" ("EXECUTOR") TAKES ACTION AFTER DEATH

In Will a person can be named "Personal Representative" to do work after a death like transfer property or money, handle debts, and do probate. Most states, most people, and this book use the older term "Executor" for this position to make understanding easier ("Executrix" was used for women long ago). If needed like if Will doesn't name anyone a judge can pick someone for this job who is then called an "Administrator", but family may argue about who should do this. Naming in Will 2 people to both act is rare due to possible disagreements and higher legal costs, and since any 1 person named should be trusted.

EXECUTOR CAN BE PAID AND ESTATE PAYS FOR THINGS

Many states let Executor ask for pay for hours worked or up to 5% of value of the estate (after debts), and this is usually fair and minor. But pay is often not asked for to avoid income tax and leave more to carry out Will gifts. Money an Executor needs like for probate fees, attorney, or repairs comes from estate assets.

EXECUTOR MUST BE ADULT, FLORIDA RESIDENT OR FAMILY, AND NOT FELON

By law an Executor must be 18 or older and either Florida resident or if out-of-state be close family of the deceased by blood or adoption (spouse, child, parent, grandparent, brother, sister, aunt, uncle, nephew, niece, or spouse of any of these). Fla. Stat. § 733.304. They also can't have felony criminal conviction, conviction for abuse or similar of an old or vulnerable person, or be clearly mentally unfit to do the job. Fla. Stat. § 733.303. Often named Executor in Will is spouse, adult child, distant family, or friend. A bank or lawyer also can be named as Executor but this is rare and they must be asked in advance and usually charge high fees.

"ALTERNATE" EXECUTOR OR GUARDIAN RARELY ADDED TO WILL

Some Wills have area to name an alternative Executor in case needed. To do this Will can be modified, like by adding "or if they are reasonably unable to serve I nominate ___ to serve". But this is rarely done since if a person is unavailable later (which is rare) a new Will can be done or judge just pick someone.

WILL CAN SAY TO SKIP COSTLY EXECUTOR "BOND"

Most Wills helpfully say no "bond" or "surety" is required for an Executor or Guardian or similar. This is insurance bought from some insurance company to insure against misconduct. But person doing a Will often doesn't want a bond since person named Executor is trusted and cost of bond uses up estate assets.

WILLS HAVE "MISCELLANEOUS" PART TO HELP WITH RARE PROBLEMS

Most Wills have a "Miscellaneous" part with many paragraphs of complex legal language to help solve some legal issues that occur in a few cases. This book's Wills have a half page of this helpful language.

CHAPTER 4
WILL GIFTS INCLUDING RESIDUE

MAIN USE OF WILL IS TO SAY GIFTS TO HAPPEN AFTER DEATH

Most people mainly use a Will to write gifts of property and money they want to happen after their death. Verbal and most written statements about this are not valid outside a Will. A Will can control what happens to property acquired after a Will was signed, so old Wills still do work. Note, families may try to agree informally to hand out small items in ways a decedent mentioned or following little notes or stickers put on items, but this is not legally property and people should not plan on using these methods and it working.

GIFTING USING SIMPLE WORDS OFTEN IS BEST

Making gifts in a Will by writing simple words is often best, using words like "I give" and "I gift". This is legally fine and avoids confusing legal words like "bequest", "devise", or "legacy" which few know.

PERSON IS MOSTLY FREE TO GIFT THEIR THINGS AS WANTED

A person is mostly free to give away their money and property as they want (like giving a child nothing).

IN WILL CAN DO "SPECIFIC GIFTS" TO GIFT PARTICULAR PROPERTY

Most Wills have "specific gifts" to gift particular things. Specific gifts can be any property, like "I give boat to Ed Poe" and "I give UBank account #845534873 to Sue Wu". If a gift is not clear the law assumes all of a kind of thing is given, like "I give jewelry to Ann Po" means all jewelry. But giving specific property can have surprises like the value of an item can greatly change or a gift may fail if property is no longer owned.

IN WILL CAN DO "GENERAL GIFTS" LIKE OF MONEY

People can do "general gifts" where what is gifted is not particular property but can be flexibly chosen, like "I give 1 of my 3 cars to Ed Po" which lets an Executor pick which car. The usual general gift is money, like "I give $5 to Ed Vu". Money gifts are easy to write, lets equal gifts be made, and are safer since person usually has money unlike specific items which might have been sold. To carry out money gifts an Executor usually just uses money in accounts or sells some property.

"RESIDUE CLAUSE" IS CATCH-ALL THAT HELPFULLY GIVES ANYTHING LEFT

Most Wills by their end have a Residue Clause to gift property or money not given or used in Will or any other way. This is often called the "catch-all" or "left-over" clause. This is covered end of this Chapter.

PERSON IN WILL GIFT USUALLY MUST SURVIVE OR GIFT DOES NOT OCCUR

Many Wills like this book's Wills say person in Will gift must survive (live past) Testator for gift to occur unless gift language says otherwise. Also, basic law usually says gifts to deceased persons have no effect. If a gift fails for non-survival a Residue Clause says where item in gift goes. If survival is not clearly required what occurs if a named recipient is dead can be confusing (partly from complex state "anti-lapse" laws). People doing Will should consider how Will gifts to people dying before Testator will usually have no effect. Many people if they see someone in a Will gift has died just re-do Will with a new name to get the gift.

SOME PEOPLE ADD "ALTERNATE BENEFICIARY" LIKE FOR SPECIAL ITEMS

A person named in a Will gift dying before Testator is rare, and if seen most people just re-do Will to add new name or let Residue Clause in Will handle it. But some people to prepare for this and maybe just for special items write in an alternate beneficiary, like, "I give Boat to Ed Wu but if they don't survive to Ben Fox".

CAN SAY IF RECIPIENT HAS DIED GIFT GOES TO "LINEAL DESCENDANTS"

A Will gift may say gift goes to person but if they don't survive to their "lineal descendants per stirpes". Descendants are person's children and grandchildren. Adding this language in case someone dies is usually not worth the time except for large gifts like of the Residue left over after other gifts. "Per stirpes" is about "how" to spread things and means "by root" or "by branch", and basically divides things so each family branch gets equal share. A family branch that died off is ignored. Most Wills use "lineal descendants" language in a Residue Clause, and it can be put in other gifts if wanted. An example shows how it works:

If Will says **"Residue to Sue Wu but if they don't survive to lineal descendants per stirpes"** this means if Sue Wu died and a son Ken Wu is living and a son Ben Wu has died but left 2 children, then Ken Wu will get 50% and Ben's 2 children each get 25%.

PROPERTY OR MONEY IN JOINT GIFT GOES TO MULTIPLE PEOPLE

The same property or money in "joint gift" can go to multiple people to each own a part interest, like "I give boat and all hats to Ann Smith and Sue Kimble" means each person owns 50% of every single item. Later people can agree how to split jointly owned things, an Executor can decide, or a sale can be held. If person in joint gift has died their part of gift usually doesn't occur so that part transfers by Residue Clause.

GIFT BENEFICIARIES CAN GET PERCENTAGE RATHER THAN EQUAL SHARE

If Will gift goes to several people the law assumes equal shares, but if wanted percentages can be put, like "I give boat 91% to Ed Wu and 9% to Jo Po". Often a Will Residue Clause is gifted using percentages.

CONDITIONS ON GIFTS ARE RARE DUE TO HUGE PROBLEMS

Conditions on gifts, like "to get $90 Ann Smith must diet 1 year", can cause huge legal problems like delay for years, long hearings, and high legal costs to lawyers. Conditions are rarely put on gifts.

HELPFUL LAWS OFTEN REQUIRE PERSON SURVIVE 120 HOURS TO GET GIFT

State laws often say person dying within 120 hours of someone is deemed to have not survived them for Will gifts or similar, and a Will need not say this itself. This avoids having to know exact time people died if close like in 1 accident, and avoids item going from 1 person to 2nd person who might quickly die and needs probate before item can go to final 3rd person.

CAN LEAVE PARTS OF WILL BLANK OR WRITE THINGS LIKE "SKIPPED"

A person can skip Will parts by leaving them blank, writing things like "SKIPPED" or "NONE", or using a computer to delete gift clauses. Judges and others do not care about neatness or empty spaces in Wills.

MUST SUFFICIENTLY DESCRIBE PROPERTY AND NAMES IN WILL

NAMES IN WILL GIFTS ARE FAIRLY EASY TO DO

Names in Will gifts just must be detailed enough so people who knew decedent can tell who likely was meant and testify if asked. Gifts to family often just use first and last name, and part names and nicknames are often fine. Detail can be added if confusion is likely, for example "maid Sue Smith" or "golf pal Ed Wu". It is assumed a person gifts to people they know, so it's OK to use common names unless 2 friends or family have same name. Names are not needed if confusion won't occur, like fine is "I give $5 to each of my sons". To avoid confusion some add "also known as" or "a/k/a" like "I give boat to John Kent a/k/a Lucky Kent".

NAMING GROUP OR CHARITY IN WILL GIFT IS FAIRLY EASY

Charity, company, or other group can get a Will gift, but an unofficial group that filed no official papers is not enough. It must be described in Will so people who knew decedent can tell what likely was meant, like probably fine is "Food Shelf in Maple, Florida". People often phone to ask for charity's name to put in Will. A government like city, state, or agency can get a Will gift, like "I give $10 to Polk, FL city library" or "I give $50 to City of Pine, FL". Will gifts face no income tax so there are no tax benefit in Will gifts to a charity.

DESCRIPTIONS OF PROPERTY IN WILL GIFTS FAIRLY EASY TO DO

Gifted property just must be described so people who knew decedent can say what likely is meant and if asked testify. This is easy as people rarely own similar items, so fine is "I give boat and big table to Ed Mo". It's usually fine to use category or list (like "clothes" and "blue chair and gold lamp"). Using just location of items is risky as judges ignore this if putting stuff in locations seems used to control gifting and not for plain life reason (so "all I put in desk" and "furniture in shed" might be ignored). Financial assets can use simple words, like "Wells Fargo accounts" or "stocks", but details help, like "Fidelity account #803434353212515".

DESCRIBING REAL PROPERTY IS HARDER SO OFTEN USE RESIDUE OR TITLE

For real property, Will gifts by street address or plain words are often fine, like "I give 28 Ivy St., Fox, FL to Su Wu" or "I give cabin in Lake Co., FL to Ed Po". Gifts by address or plain words do by law include all buildings and fixtures there and nearby land not separated by roads, but not other land. A "legal description" is best but long (like "Lot 11, Block 8 of Po's Addition to Hud, FL according to plat in land office in Bear Co."). To make it easier many people use the Residue Clause to gift real property, or put 2nd person on land title.

SIMPLE WILL IS OFTEN BEST AND PEOPLE MOSTLY GIFT BY RESIDUE CLAUSE

People may consider doing complex and detailed Will but simple Will is often best leaving parts blank.

If there is a spouse often people do a few small gifts to friends and other family, then use Residue Clause of Will to gift spouse the Residue, and then name a few fallback persons in the Residue Clause.

If there is no spouse often people do a few small gifts, then name some family or friends to get Residue.

A parent with young children if married to other parent often gifts Residue to them, and as fallback gifts Residue to the young children. Or if not married to other parent a person often gifts the Residue to the young children and name other parent "Guardian of the Property" to help manage the children's things.

RESIDUE CLAUSE

"RESIDUE CLAUSE" IS CATCH-ALL THAT HELPS GIFTS ANYTHING LEFT

Wills by their end have a Residue Clause to gift property or money not given or used in other ways to persons named here. Many people do most their giving this way as it skips need to describe things and has less legal risk. If after applying a Residue Clause anything is left (which happens in rare cases) then closest "heirs" get things which is closest family like child, parent, brother/sister, grandparent, aunt/uncle, and cousins. People can gift in Will the Residue to multiple people by percentages, which of course should add to 100%.

USUAL RESIDUE CLAUSE HAS 2 PARTS

A short 2 part Residue Clause is usual and is used in this book's Wills, and it has:

1) 1st space to name 1 or more persons to get things if they survive Testator (many name a spouse or closest family here), and if several people are named but only some survive then survivors get things, and

2) 2nd space to name persons to get things if all in 1st space don't survive (so these are "fallbacks") (many name next family or friends here), and if person in 2nd space died their descendants get their share.

EXAMPLE OF 2 PART RESIDUE CLAUSE:

"RESIDUE CLAUSE: I give money and property not gifted earlier:

A) to _____my husband John Paul Doe_____ if they survive me, then

B) to ____Sam Doe my son, Beth Wu my daughter, and Greta Fisher my friend____ and if any of those just named do not survive me their part goes to their lineal descendants, per stirpes."

In this example if John Paul Doe has survived then he gets things. But if John Paul Doe hasn't survived and also Sam Doe hasn't survived and he left 2 daughters, then those 2 daughters split the 1/3 share of Sam Doe so get 1/6 each and other 2 persons in second part Beth Wu and Greta Fisher get 1/3 each.

SOME PEOPLE RE-WRITE RESIDUE CLAUSE TO HAVE 1 PART

A normal Residue Clause of 2 parts is often fine, and basically person put in 1st part usually gets things. A small fraction of people may want to do a "Simple Residue Clause" which has a clause of 1 part to gift to group more equally. If person named in this new Residue Clause has died their descendants get their part. People with no spouse and no children are likelier to do this change, but even they often don't bother and just use this book's Will forms as is. See Example below for exact words to add if people want this change.

EXAMPLE OF SIMPLE RESIDUE CLAUSE:

"RESIDUE CLAUSE: The rest, residue, and remainder of my estate, property of any kind and nature, and anything I have an interest in, I give to __Adam Doe_ and _Beth Wu__ who survive me, and to lineal descendants per stirpes of any person just named who did not survive me."

In this example if Adam hasn't survived but had 2 children they each get 25%, and if Beth Wu survived she gets 50%. Or if Beth Wu also hadn't survived and had 5 kids they split her part and each gets 10%.

CHAPTER 5
DEBT, MARRIAGE, AND YOUNG CHILD ISSUES

DEBT, MARRIAGE, AND YOUNG CHILD CAN CAUSE ISSUES

This Chapter deals with debt issues , marriage issues , and young child issues . People can skip the parts of this Chapter they think will not apply to them.

DEBT ISSUES

PAYING DECEDENT'S DEBTS MAY USE UP RESOURCES AND REDUCE GIFTS

Creditors owed by decedent can ask judge to be paid from decedent's money and property before Will gifts are carried out. But if decedent had under $50,000 of money and things plus house any creditors often do not bother, for reasons explained below. Resources to pay debts first come from things in Will Residue, then general gifts like of money, and then specific gifts. Some debts like for probate, attorney for probate, funeral, and medical debts have priority to be paid first. Spouse or family are not usually personally liable to pay decedent's debts unless they guaranteed or co-signed. People should consider how paying debts may use up things leaving less to carry out Will gifts. People can research their own state.

BEFORE DEBTS ARE PAID MAY COME SOME FAMILY RIGHTS

Most states say spouse or minor children have "family rights" they can claim before debts are paid, which can help family get some things if decedent had debts. Some states say $10,000 for "year living allowance", $30,000 of "exempt property", and other rights exist. Family rights use up money and property so if used less may be left to do Will gifts. Creditors know of family rights so often don't seek payment if told decedent had little except a house, and if their calls are wisely ignored by family. People can research their state.

"HOMESTEAD EXEMPTION" PROTECTS HOME FOR FAMILY FROM DEBTS

"Homestead" laws in most states say decedent's creditors can't seek payment by foreclosing and selling decedent's house if decedent's spouse or children under 18 are there (unless equity is big, like $1 million). Homestead laws also often say spouse or minor children get ownership of decedent's house (or use for their life in some states) if decedent owned it and regardless of Will gift giving it to other people. Due to all this most people give spouse or if no spouse minor children the house by Will or by naming them on land title.

Florida homestead law is similar to basic rule with few special details. State law and Florida Constitution say house or mobile home owned and lived in and 1/2 acre in city (160 acres in country) go to any surviving spouse or minor kids no matter what Will says. See Fla. Stat. § 732.401(1). If spouse and minor kids are there they split things and spouse gets house for life (a "life estate") and kids get "remainder" when spouse dies (or spouse can elect a 50/50 split by sale). If children are all 18 a Will can give spouse all of house, but if a Will forgets to do this then adult children get a remainder interest. But homestead rights don't overrule joint ownership so if house is owned by 2 people on the title the surviving person (often a spouse) usually gets the property. Of course a normal mortgage later can be foreclosed if not paid monthly by spouse or kids.

USUALLY SECURED DEBTS LIKE MORTGAGE OR VEHICLE LIEN NOT PAID OFF

Usually laws say secured debts like house mortgage or car lien are not paid off after death but remain,

even if a Will says generally to pay debts. This book's Wills in the Miscellaneous section also say this.
This avoids using most of decedent's things on secured debts so more is left to carry out all the Will gifts.
People who get a Will gift of house or car must usually later make monthly payments of any mortgage or lien
to avoid foreclosure or repossession. If Testator wants to pay off secured debts they can a) in Will also give
a person enough cash to pay them, or b) add order to pay in Will (like "I order mortgage on cabin paid off").

MARRIAGE ISSUES

MOST STATES USE "SEPARATE PROPERTY LAW" FOR SPOUSES

Most states including Florida use "Separate Property" law saying married person mostly owns money
and property separately, and usually own their own income and profits and also accounts and property in
their names. Due to this a spouse is mostly free to sell during life their things, or gift in their Will their things
with some exceptions as this book explains. But joint ownership by 2 spouses can arise by agreement,
paying half a purchase price, and also many spouses do paperwork to own a house jointly.

"COMMUNITY PROPERTY" LAW APPLIES IN OTHER STATES FOR SPOUSES

There are 9 states mostly in West and South USA that use "Community Property" law for spouses.
This says if a married person lives in these states most property or money gotten is usually owned 50/50
by spouses as "Community Property" if it relates to activities during the marriage (like from labor or
wages, or active management of a small business) or if bought or improved with Community Property.
Community Property law states are Arizona, California, Louisiana, Idaho, Nevada, New Mexico, Texas,
Washington, and Wisconsin. Most people avoid these issues unless moving to or from these states.

"JOINT WILL" SIGNED BY BOTH SPOUSES IS NOT RECOMMENDED

Some couples sign 1 "Joint Will" written by a lawyer saying spouses gives all to the other if they die first,
then saying last living spouse gives to all children equally, and usually it says a spouse may not change this.
Joint Wills are not recommended and banned in some states and most people dislike how restrictive it is.

SPOUSE CAN SEEK "ELECTIVE SHARE" SO USUALLY GIVE SPOUSE 50%

Most states using Separate Property law (like Florida) for fairness give spouse if unhappy with what
a Will gifts them a right to choose (elect) an "Elective Share" of their spouse's property and money instead.
Many states say an Elective Share is 20% rising to 50% with time up to 20 years, though Florida skips this
and basically gives a 30% share of the other spouse's things. To avoid tricks an Elective Share by law can
cover more like anything spouse gave away recently, things not owned but controlled by spouse, and more.
If an Elective Share is used then any Will gifts to the electing spouse are not done, but Will gifts to other
people are carried out like normal unless the property and money is needed to satisfy the Elective Share.
Because of all this usually a married person gifts by Will and other ways mostly to their spouse (often about
50% and the family house) to avoid a spouse being upset and using an Elective Share.

16

YOUNG CHILD ISSUES

CAN NAME "GUARDIAN OF THE PERSON" TO CARE FOR CHILD

If person dies with minor child under 18 the other natural or adopted parent (but not step-parent) automatically takes over daily care (and related issues like school, discipline, and health care) unless the other parent is unavailable or proven unfit in court which is rare. But just in case needed a parent in Will can name someone as "Guardian of the Person" to do this daily care for a child.

MOST NAME HEALTHY RELATIVE OR FRIEND AS "GUARDIAN OF THE PERSON"

Since naming other parent is pointless (they take over if fit and available) most Wills name as Guardian of the Person a healthy friend or relative over age 18 in case other parent is later unavailable or proven unfit. If no Will names person then family can have judge say who is best for this with closest family usually chosen, but it can lead to arguments. Preference of last living parent has more weight. Naming 2 persons to both serve like a married couple is rare since they may argue and any 1 person named should be trusted.

CAN NAME "GUARDIAN OF THE PROPERTY" TO MANAGE ASSETS OF CHILD

A child until 18 legally can't easily manage money or property, so in Will a person can be named as "Guardian of the Property" for rare case young child gets property or money. This person would manage money and property of child and decide what school, health care, living costs, and more to pay for them. Other states often call this "Guardian of the Estate" or "Conservator". Anyone including a Guardian that is giving child a home or necessities can ask to be paid back from child's money and property a fair amount. Judges often hold a yearly hearing looking for misuse or misconduct which can cause some hassles.

MOST NAME OTHER PARENT AS "GUARDIAN OF THE PROPERTY"

Usually 1 parent will be still alive most people in Will name other parent as Guardian of the Property because they know best what spending is needed, care about child, and may argue with anyone else. But a person not the other parent can be named as Guardian of the Property (like a relative or friend), maybe if other parent is unstable or bad with money. If no Will names someone or if they are unavailable (which is rare) family can have judge pick a person but this can cause family arguments. Having 2 persons for this like a married couple is rare as the 2 may argue and any 1 person named should be trusted.

GUARDIAN MUST BE ADULT, FLORIDA RESIDENT OR FAMILY, AND NOT FELON

To be Guardian person must be at least 18 and Florida resident or if out of state be certain close family of child (parent, grandparent, brother, sister, uncle, aunt, niece, nephew, or spouse of these). Fla. Stat. § 744.309. They also can't have felony criminal conviction, conviction for abuse or neglect or similar, or be clearly unfit.

PICKING GUARDIANS RARELY MATTERS DESPITE PARENTS WORRYING

Naming Guardians rarely matters. A study shows just 0.2% of children had 2 parents die to be left totally parentless and likely need Guardians. *Socioeconomic Parent Mortality, Census Bureau 288.* It is also rare for young child to get property or money rather than a parent left alive. People also shouldn't worry much about a named Guardian dying, this is rare and judge has power to name someone, but some worried people name an alternate, like by adding "or if they are reasonably unable to serve I nominate _____ to serve".

17

CHAPTER 6
BASIC IDEAS ABOUT HEALTH CARE FORMS

SOME BASIC IDEAS HELP USE HEALTH CARE FORMS

■ By law people control their health care unless "incapacitated" by inability to a) <u>communicate</u> verbally or by notes, b) be <u>rational</u>, or c) be <u>conscious.</u> Unless incapacitated people just tell doctor their wishes, or maybe family or friend is made Agent to help do this. Most people keep control of their health care till death or till no big treatment options remain to choose, but people worry they may be the exception so do health care forms.

■ Parents <u>do</u> have power over health care of <u>child under 18</u>. And family like spouse or children can make emergency decisions for <u>older incapacitated person</u> but must rush to judge if no form names them agent.

■ In form a person can <u>name an "Agent"</u> to help make health decisions or take control later if needed, and naming an Agent often a spouse or adult child can avoid family later having to rush to get power from judge.

■ In form person can give <u>written instructions doctors, family, and any Agent must obey</u>, but many skip this since it's hard to write to cover all possibilities, unclear instructions can be a legal problem, and most people just trust family or agent to wisely consider many factors. People can give instructions but skip an agent.

■ **Young people** often skip health care forms since they rarely are very ill. But some **married people** do a form to name spouse as Agent. **People 19-25** sometimes do form to name parents as Agents.

■ **Older people** over 40 often do form naming Agent but many skip instructions to not limit the freedom of their agent, but people with strong wishes might write instructions carefully maybe with a doctor's help.

■ Pain relief like pain drugs and comfort care is usually given even if forms say to stop or limit other care.

■ <u>Most people do the main long health care form, mostly to name Agent just in case this is ever needed</u>. Usually only sickest or oldest people do other health care forms, like under 5% in some states.

■ For <u>rare</u> cases person likely will be <u>incapacitated</u> and <u>stopping care an issue due to worsening health</u>:

-- most people <u>do nothing special and trust family or Agent to decide</u> on stopping care based on changing complex factors like pain, cost, hassle, suffering and time of treatment, beliefs, and chances of recovery;

-- a few people do extreme legal document sometimes called a "Living Will" to <u>block most health care</u> but only <u>if **later** doctors think person has irrevocable terminal condition</u> and <u>care likely won't help</u> (mostly done if very old or sick, family are too delicate or stubborn, and no wise friend can be Agent to say when to stop);

-- a few people do extreme legal document often called a "Do-Not-Resuscitate" to **starting immediately** <u>block some health care</u> listed (on a very short form) like C.P.R. (mostly done if very old or sick, family are too delicate or stubborn, and no wise friend can be made Agent to say when to stop medical treatment).

CHAPTER 7
FORM 1: LAST WILL AND TESTAMENT (STANDARD)

FORM 1 IS A STANDARD WILL THAT IS FLEXIBLE WITH NO GUARDIANS

Form 1 is a standard Will that is flexible and is the Will form most people use. It has no part about guardians or similar so is usually for person with no child under age 18.

WILL IN FORM 1 HAS BASIC LAYOUT WITH SEVERAL PARTS

The Will at its start has place for person doing the Will (Testator) to write their name and county.

The 1st paragraph, "Gifts", has many spaces to make either specific gifts of particular property or general gifts like of money. People can delete, copy and paste to add more, or leave blank these gift lines.

The 2nd paragraph, "Gifts Of Tangible Personal Property By Separate Writings", says to follow any separate writings done apart and later than the Will that gift tangible personal property.

The 3rd paragraph, "Residue", has a Residue Clause to gift property and money left after other Will parts to those persons named here.

The 4th paragraph, "Administration", has space to name a "Personal Representative" to handle legal and other matters after death.

The 5th paragraph, "Miscellaneous", has sentences of legal language to help avoid certain legal issues.

Last is a paragraph for person doing Will to date and sign, and 2 witnesses to sign and give addresses.

USUAL RESIDUE CLAUSE HAS 2 PLACES TO NAME PERSONS TO GET THINGS

In "Residue Clause" of Will anything left after other Will parts is gifted to persons who are named here. Many people use a Residue Clause to gift most things. In the Residue Clause in this book's Will there is:
 1) a 1st space to name 1 or more persons to get the residue, and if any named here have not survived
    and died before the Will maker then any other persons named here take their share,
 2) a 2nd space to name people to get things if all in 1st space died before Will maker (these are "fallbacks")
    and if any people named here didn't survive their shares go to "lineal descendants" like their children.
Most people name in 1st space a spouse or closest family or closest friends, and in 2nd space next closest family or friends. This may seem complicated but usually those in 1st area of Residue Clause get things.

TESTATOR SIGNS AND DECLARES IT IS A WILL AND 2 WITNESSES SIGN

A Will after being filled out by computer or by hand in pen or pencil (except bits intentionally left blank) then should be signed by person doing Will ("Testator") before 2 witnesses at least age 18 who sign too. It is usually best to use witnesses not getting gifts in Will and not named Executor or Guardian in the Will. For signing use pen or marker with permanent ink not pencil, and Testator and 2 witnesses should be in same room and see each other sign. Witnesses only read the 1 paragraph they sign and not the full Will. It is not required but some Testators say to witnesses a thing like "This is my Will" and may hold it up, and also Testators may chat a bit with witnesses to try to show they are of sound mind and not being forced.

LAST WILL AND TESTAMENT

I, _____, of _____ County, Florida, do revoke all prior Wills, Testaments, and Codicils, and do make, publish, and declare this to be my Will. When doing this I am of sound mind and under no duress or undue influence.

1. GIFTS. I give these gifts in this Will, but to get a gift in this section the recipient must survive me except as otherwise stated below.

I give _____ to _____.

I give _____ to _____.

I give _____ to _____.

I give _____ to _____.

I give _____ to _____.

I give _____ to _____.

I give _____ to _____.

I give _____ to _____.

I give _____ to _____.

I give _____ to _____.

I give _____ to _____.

I give _____ to _____.

2. GIFTS OF TANGIBLE PERSONAL PROPERTY BY SEPARATE WRITINGS.
I may give tangible personal property by writings separate from a Will as allowed by state law, but writings not found within 90 days of my death shall be canceled and of no effect.

3. RESIDUE. I give the rest and residue and remainder of my estate, my money and property of any kind and nature, and anything I have an interest in so long as it was not transferred by other Will provisions (all of which is called the "residue"), as follows:

   a) to _____ who survive me with persons just named who survive me taking the share of non-survivors, then

   b) to _____ and if any of those just named do not survive me their part goes to their lineal descendants per stirpes.

4. ADMINISTRATION. I name and appoint _____ as Personal Representative including for me, my Will, and my estate.

5. MISCELLANEOUS. The following applies to this Will and generally.

   Priority of Will gifts of the same type is based on the order they are written.

   The words "give" and "gift" also means a devise, bequest, grant, legacy, or similar.

   If gift or gift section mentions survival, survive, or surviving then survival is an absolute condition and anti-lapse laws or similar have no effect.

   In this document no unfilled part is a mistake and residue spaces may be left blank.

   Any failure to make gifts to family including children is intentional and not a mistake.

   No gift or transfer made during life reduces or offsets a Will gift unless during my life I expressly called it a "loan" or "advancement".

   Use of particular gender shall include other genders, reference to singular or plural shall be interchangeable, and "they" may be singular or plural.

   If context permits the terms Personal Representative, Executor, and Administrator shall be seen as interchangeable as if all were written, and if context permits Guardian of the Property is interchangeable with Guardian of the Estate and Conservator.

   Any Personal Representative may anytime pay or settle claims or debts they in their sole discretion find proper or helpful to pay, but I specifically say any secured debts including mortgages or liens on real property or vehicles should not be paid off unless parts of this Will specify it.

   I give any person named or acting as Personal Representative the fullest power and discretion allowed by state law, and I grant them all powers that may be conferred on Personal Representatives by state law.

   Any Personal Representative shall not be required to render and file annual accountings with respect to property or money including in relation to my Will or estate.

   I authorize informal probate of my estate and Will and also administrative probate if any Personal Representative chooses, and any Personal Representative may act

independently in all ways without supervision including from any court or judge.

I give any Personal Representative authority to lease, sell, mortgage, convey, or retain property of mine in such manner and time they deem in the best interest, helpful, or proper.

The residue includes lapsed or failed gifts, insurance paid to estate, inheritances owed me, and property I had a power of appointment or testamentary disposition over.

If in Florida or other place a Conservator, Administrator, Guardian of the Property, or any other fiduciary is needed for a child of mine or their estate or property, or for any other person, then I appoint for that the person named Personal Representative above.

Any Personal Representative, Guardian, Executor, Conservator, or fiduciary under this Will or otherwise, shall qualify and serve without bond, surety, security, or similar, including despite their place of residence or lack of relationship to any state or country.

TESTATOR

IN WITNESS WHEREOF, I, _____, sign, publish, and declare this instrument as my Will, this ___ day of _____, 20__.

_____
Testator signature

WITNESSES

The foregoing instrument was signed by the Testator and Testator declared it to be the Testator's Will, which signing and declaration was made in the presence of us the witnesses, and we do now sign our names in this document below as witnesses at the request and in the presence of the Testator and presence of each other on this ___ day of _____, 20__.

_____   _____
Witness signature   Witness address

_____   _____
Witness signature   Witness address

CHAPTER 8
FORM 2: LAST WILL AND TESTAMENT (GUARDIANS)

FORM 2 IS BASIC WILL WITH GUARDIANS CLAUSE FOR THOSE NEEDING THIS

Form 2 is a Will with Guardians clause for people with child under 18 or caring for incapacitated person.

WILL IN FORM 2 HAS BASIC LAYOUT WITH SEVERAL PARTS

The Will at its start has place for person doing the Will (Testator) to write their name and county.

The 1st paragraph, "Gifts", has many spaces to make either specific gifts of particular property or general gifts like of money. People can delete, copy and paste to add more, or leave blank these gift lines.

The 2nd paragraph, "Gifts Of Tangible Personal Property By Separate Writings", says to follow any separate writings done apart and later than the Will that gift tangible personal property.

The 3rd paragraph, "Residue", has a Residue Clause to gift property and money left after other Will parts to those persons named here.

The 4th paragraph, "Administration", has space to name a "Personal Representative" to handle legal and other matters after death.

The 5th paragraph, "Guardians", lets "Guardian of the Person" be named to care for child or similar person, and also "Guardian of the Property" be named to manage such persons property and money.

The 6th paragraph, "Miscellaneous", has sentences of legal language to help avoid certain legal issues.

Last is a paragraph for person doing Will to date and sign, and 2 witnesses to sign and give addresses.

USUAL RESIDUE CLAUSE HAS 2 PLACES TO NAME PERSONS TO GET THINGS

In "Residue Clause" of Will anything left after other Will parts is gifted to persons who are named here. Many people use a Residue Clause to gift most things. In the Residue Clause in this book's Will there is:
  1) a 1st space to name 1 or more persons to get the residue, and if any named here have not survived and died before the Will maker then any other persons named here take their share,
  2) a 2nd space to name people to get things if all in 1st space died before Will maker (these are "fallbacks") and if any people named here didn't survive their shares go to "lineal descendants" like their children.
Most people name in 1st space a spouse or closest family or closest friends, and in 2nd space next closest family or friends. This may seem complicated but usually those in 1st area of Residue Clause get things.

TESTATOR SIGNS AND DECLARES IT IS A WILL AND 2 WITNESSES SIGN

A Will after being filled out by computer or by hand in pen or pencil (except bits intentionally left blank) then should be signed by person doing Will ("Testator") before 2 witnesses at least age 18 who sign too. It is usually best to use witnesses not getting gifts in Will and not named Executor or Guardian in the Will. For signing use pen or marker with permanent ink not pencil, and Testator and 2 witnesses should be in same room and see each other sign. Witnesses only read the 1 paragraph they sign and not the full Will. It is not required but some Testators say to witnesses a thing like "This is my Will" and may hold it up, and also Testators may chat a bit with witnesses to try to show they are of sound mind and not being forced.

LAST WILL AND TESTAMENT

I, _____, of _____ County, Florida, do revoke all prior Wills, Testaments, and Codicils, and do make, publish, and declare this to be my Will. When doing this I am of sound mind and under no duress or undue influence.

1. GIFTS. I give these gifts in this Will, but to get a gift in this section the recipient must survive me except as otherwise stated below.

I give _____ to _____.

I give _____ to _____.

I give _____ to _____.

I give _____ to _____.

I give _____ to _____.

I give _____ to _____.

I give _____ to _____.

I give _____ to _____.

I give _____ to _____.

I give _____ to _____.

I give _____ to _____.

I give _____ to _____.

2. GIFTS OF TANGIBLE PERSONAL PROPERTY BY SEPARATE WRITINGS.
I may give tangible personal property by writings separate from a Will as allowed by state law, but writings not found within 90 days of my death shall be canceled and of no effect.

3. RESIDUE. I give the rest and residue and remainder of my estate, my money and property of any kind and nature, and anything I have an interest in so long as it was not transferred by other Will provisions (all of which is called the "residue"), as follows:

   a) to _____ who survive me with persons just named who survive me taking the share of non-survivors, then

   b) to _____ and if any of those just named do not survive me their part goes to their lineal descendants per stirpes.

4. ADMINISTRATION. I name and appoint _____ as Personal Representative including for me, my Will, and my estate.

5. GUARDIANS. I name and nominate _____ as Guardian of the Person of any minor child of mine or other person without full legal capacity. I also name and nominate _____ as Guardian of the Property of any minor child of mine or other person without full legal capacity, and this person I name should be guardian for their money, property, and estate.

6. MISCELLANEOUS. The following applies to this Will and generally.

   Priority of Will gifts of the same type is based on the order they are written.

   The words "give" and "gift" also means a devise, bequest, grant, legacy, or similar.

   If gift or gift section mentions survival, survive, or surviving then survival is an absolute condition and anti-lapse laws or similar have no effect.

   In this document no unfilled part is a mistake and residue spaces may be left blank.

   Any failure to make gifts to family including children is intentional and not a mistake.

   No gift or transfer made during life reduces or offsets a Will gift unless during my life I expressly called it a "loan" or "advancement".

   Use of particular gender shall include other genders, reference to singular or plural shall be interchangeable, and "they" may be singular or plural.

   If context permits the terms Personal Representative, Executor, and Administrator shall be seen as interchangeable as if all were written, and if context permits Guardian of the Property is interchangeable with Guardian of the Estate and Conservator.

   Any Personal Representative may anytime pay or settle claims or debts they in their sole discretion find proper or helpful to pay, but I specifically say any secured debts including mortgages or liens on real property or vehicles should not be paid off unless parts of this Will specify it.

   I give any person named or acting as Personal Representative the fullest power and

discretion allowed by state law, and I grant them all powers that may be conferred on Personal Representatives by state law.

Any Personal Representative shall not be required to render and file annual accountings with respect to property or money including in relation to my Will or estate.

I authorize informal probate of my estate and Will and also administrative probate if any Personal Representative chooses, and any Personal Representative may act independently in all ways without supervision including from any court or judge.

I give any Personal Representative authority to lease, sell, mortgage, convey, or retain property of mine in such manner and time they deem in the best interest, helpful, or proper.

The residue includes lapsed or failed gifts, insurance paid to estate, inheritances owed me, and property I had a power of appointment or testamentary disposition over.

If in Florida or other place a Conservator, Administrator, Guardian of the Property, or any other fiduciary is needed for a child of mine or their estate or property, or for any other person, then I appoint for that the person named Personal Representative above.

Any Personal Representative, Guardian, Executor, Conservator, or fiduciary under this Will or otherwise, shall qualify and serve without bond, surety, security, or similar, including despite their place of residence or lack of relationship to any state or country.

TESTATOR

IN WITNESS WHEREOF, I, _____, sign, publish, and declare this instrument as my Will, this ___ day of _____, 20__.

_____
Testator signature

WITNESSES

The foregoing instrument was signed by the Testator and Testator declared it to be the Testator's Will, which signing and declaration was made in the presence of us the witnesses, and we do now sign our names in this document below as witnesses at the request and in the presence of the Testator and presence of each other on this ___ day of _____, 20__.

_____   _____
Witness signature   Witness address

_____   _____
Witness signature   Witness address

CHAPTER 9
FORM 3: SELF-PROVING AFFIDAVIT

FORM CAN BE DONE TO SUPPORT A WILL

The "Self-Proving Affidavit" form is optional but can be done with a Will to reduce later legal work. This is a statutory form found in law to use if wanted at Florida Statutes § 732.503.

FORM SAVES LATER WORK OF SHOWING WILL WAS PROPERLY SIGNED

A Self-Proving Affidavit "proves" Will was signed by the Testator doing Will and 2 witnesses. If this form is not done after death a little work is required to get testimony of either a) the 2 witnesses to Will signing, b) persons familiar with signatures of people, or c) handwriting expert. And if this form is not done there is bit more risk Will is not legally followed. But of people doing Wills about half skip doing a Self-Proving Affidavit mostly due to hassle of finding notary on top of 2 witnesses each time a Will is done or re-done, and since it just saves a little later work after a death of people likely happy to testify to gets things through the Will. Some states have no Self-Proving Affidavit form and manage to do fine without it.

FORM IS DONE BY TESTATOR AND 2 WITNESSES SIGNING BEFORE NOTARY

For Self-Proving Affidavit form a notary (also called "notary public") must see Testator and 2 witnesses sign form, and then notary signs and often stamps form (they "notarize" it). Some officials can also do this. A notary can be found and asked to help at banks, insurance agents, some government offices, libraries, courts, or by looking in phonebook, and they tend to help existing customers or people who pay small fee. The Self-Proving Affidavit form is often done within minutes of when Will is signed, but it also can be done anytime later (even many months) when Testator and 2 witnesses can arrange to all meet with a notary. Once done the Self-Proving Affidavit if often kept with the Will.

SELF-PROVING AFFIDAVIT

(Florida Statutes § 732.503)

STATE OF FLORIDA

COUNTY OF _____

I,_____, Testator, declare to the officer taking my acknowledgment of this instrument, and to the subscribing witnesses, that I signed this instrument as my Will.

_____
Testator

We,_____ and _____, have been sworn by the officer signing below, and declare to that officer on our oaths that the Testator declared the instrument to be the testator's Will and signed it in our presence and that we each signed the instrument as a witness in the presence of the Testator and of each other.

_____   _____
Witness   Witness

ACKNOWLEDGED AND SUBSCRIBED before me by means of physical presence of the Testator, _____, who is (check a box) [   ] personally known to me or [   ] has produced identification in the form of _____ , and

sworn to and subscribed before me by both physically present two witnesses: _____ who is (check a box) [   ] personally known to me or [   ] has produced identification in the form of _____ , and

_____ who is (check a box) [   ] personally known to me or [   ] has produced identification in the form of _____.

Subscribed by me in the presence of the Testator and the two subscribing witnesses, by the means specified herein, all on the ___ day of _____, 20___.

_____
Notary Public: State of Florida

CHAPTER 10
FORM 4: TANGIBLE PERSONAL PROPERTY LIST

FORM LETS GIFTS OF NORMAL PROPERTY BE EASILY MADE AFTER WILL

Form lets people after Will is done easily write out more gifts of property to occur after their death. These separate lists are allowed by Florida Statutes § 732.515, and about half the states allow this. These lists are often called a "Memorandum", "Memo", or "Gift Memo".

FORM GIVES EASY QUICK WAY TO WRITE GIFTS

The List form lets person after a Will has been done write out more gifts of property to occur after their death without the hassle of doing a new Will. About 30 states including Florida allow this. For a List to be valid a Will must have been done saying this is allowed. If List and Will gift the same item then the Will is followed. People can do many List pages over time and all will count. People can sign and date a List and then slowly fill it out over the years. If several Lists gift the same item the more recently done List controls. To avoid uncertainty and delay a List not found within 90 days of death is ignored. To cancel a List rip it or throw it out, or mark it like with "X" or "void".

CAN ONLY GIFT "TANGIBLE PERSONAL PROPERTY"

The List form can gift only "tangible personal property" so tangible (touchable) things (not accounts or most investments) and not "real property" (not land or buildings). It usually can't cover "inventory" of a business, and can't cover cash or coins even if antiques. Improper property written in a form is ignored.

TO COMPLETE GIFT LIST SIGN AND DATE

To be valid a List form just must be signed and usually dated. If many pages of List forms are done they are usually kept together and paper-clipped to a Will.

TANGIBLE PERSONAL PROPERTY LIST

My Will may refer to separate writings making gifts to occur at death and I do this writing for that purpose including as allowed by Florida Statutes § 732.515.

I understand in this writing only tangible personal property can be given and also only things not specifically disposed of by Will.

I may do many pages of these writings at different times and they all should be seen as 1 document, and if any conflicts occur the more recently done page controls.

If a person getting a gift below does not survive me such gift shall lapse and instead that property passes as my Will says including by a Will residue clause.

This page if not found within 90 days of my death shall have no effect.

PROPERTY ITEMS		NAMES OF RECIPIENTS
_____	to	_____
_____	to	_____
_____	to	_____
_____	to	_____
_____	to	_____
_____	to	_____
_____	to	_____
_____	to	_____
_____	to	_____
_____	to	_____
_____	to	_____
_____	to	_____
_____	to	_____
_____	to	_____
_____	to	_____
_____	to	_____

DATE:_____   SIGNED:_____

CHAPTER 11
FORM 5: DESIGNATION OF HEALTH CARE SURROGATE

FORM CAN NAME SURROGATE TO HELP CONTROL HEALTH CARE

Form lets person name someone as "Surrogate" to make health care decisions in case person doing form is later incapacitated. This form is a statutory form found in law at Florida Statutes § 765.203. Many people do this 1 health care form and skip other health care forms.

CAN NAME "SURROGATE" TO HAVE POWER OVER HEALTH CARE IF NEEDED

Form lets a person name someone "Health Care Surrogate" to have power over medical decisions if person is later incapacitated and can't communicate or understand well enough to control own health care. Often named is spouse, other family, or friend. Naming a family member in form can avoid them the hassle of going to a judge to get power in some situations. The form has a spot to name an "Alternate" Surrogate to act if first Surrogate isn't able to, but many people skip this as rarely needed.

FORM HAS A FEW OPTIONS TO INITIAL

The form in this book has some options to initial if a person wants. The form also has been modified to have a couple options that most lawyers find helpful which are in the "Specific Instructions" part of form. The form has a spot to initial if Surrogate may stop "life prolonging" care which is extreme action and sort of what Living Will covers, and some people choose to give this major power. The form also has spot to initial to say Surrogate must obey any other health care documents a person did, and most people do not initial this since they trust their Surrogate and don't want to limit them.

SIGN FORM WITH 2 WITNESSES

To complete form person doing form signs and then 2 witnesses sign. Witnesses must be at least 18 and at least 1 can't be spouse or blood relative of person doing form. A person can keep form until needed, or many people immediately hand it to the Surrogate. The form usually should be shown to any doctor or facility that may give care to make it part of person's medical file to be followed. To cancel form a person can rip it up or say or write it is canceled to Surrogate, and maybe inform all places who saw the old form.

DESIGNATION OF HEALTH CARE SURROGATE
(Florida Statutes § 765.203)

I, _____, designate as my **health care surrogate** under s. 765.202, Florida Statutes:

Name:_____ Phone:_____

Address: _____

If my health care surrogate is not willing, able, or reasonably available to perform his or her duties, I designate as my **alternate health care surrogate**:

Name:_____ Phone:_____

Address: _____

INSTRUCTIONS FOR HEALTH CARE

I authorize my health care surrogate to:

_____
(initial here)

Receive any of my health information, whether oral or recorded in any form medium, that:

1. Is created or received by a health care provider, health care facility, health plan, public health authority, employer, life insurer, school or university, or health care clearinghouse; and
2. Relates to my past, present, or future physical or mental health or condition; the provision of health care to me; or the past, present, or future payment for the provision of health care to me.

I further authorize my health care surrogate to:

_____
(initial here)

Make all health care decisions for me, which means he or she has the authority to:

1. Provide informed consent, refusal of consent, or withdrawal of consent to any and all of my health care, including life-prolonging procedures.
2. Apply on my behalf for private, public, government, or veterans' benefits to defray the cost of health care.
3. Access my health information reasonably necessary for the health care surrogate to make decisions involving my health care and to apply for benefits for me.
4. Decide to make an anatomical gift pursuant to part V of chapter 765, Florida Statutes.

SPECIFIC INSTRUCTIONS AND RESTRICTIONS

_____
(initial here)

I hereby require my surrogate to direct my physicians **to comply with any valid Living Will, Directive to Physicians, or similar** document which I may have heretofore executed or which I may hereafter execute. My surrogate is not authorized to direct my physician in a manner which would contradict any such valid Living Will, Directive to Physicians, or similar document.

_____
(initial here)

My surrogate **may provide consent for the withholding or withdrawing of life prolonging procedures** (as long as my unborn child or children are not considered viable as defined in Section 390.011(12) of the Florida Statutes).

While I have decisionmaking capacity, my wishes are controlling and my physicians and health care providers **must clearly communicate to me the treatment plan** or any change to the treatment plan prior to its implementation.

To the extent I am capable of understanding, my health care surrogate **shall keep me reasonably informed** of all decisions that he or she has made on my behalf and matters concerning me.

THIS HEALTH CARE SURROGATE DESIGNATION IS NOT AFFECTED BY MY SUBSEQUENT INCAPACITY EXCEPT AS PROVIDED IN CHAPTER 765, FLORIDA STATUTES.

PURSUANT TO SECTION SECTION 765.104, FLORIDA STATUTES, I UNDERSTAND THAT I MAY, AT ANY TIME WHILE I RETAIN MY CAPACITY, REVOKE OR AMEND THIS DESIGNATION BY:

(1) SIGNING A WRITTEN AND DATED INSTRUMENT WHICH EXPRESSES MY INTENT TO AMEND OR REVOKE THIS DESIGNATION;

(2) PHYSICALLY DESTROYING THIS DESIGNATION THROUGH MY OWN ACTION OR BY THAT OF ANOTHER PERSON IN MY PRESENCE AND UNDER MY DIRECTION;

(3) VERBALLY EXPRESSING MY INTENTION TO AMEND OR REVOKE THIS DESIGNATION; OR

(4) SIGNING A NEW DESIGNATION THAT IS MATERIALLY DIFFERENT FROM THIS DESIGNATION.

MY HEALTH CARE SURROGATE'S AUTHORITY BECOMES EFFECTIVE **WHEN MY PRIMARY PHYSICIAN DETERMINES** THAT I AM UNABLE TO MAKE MY OWN HEALTH CARE DECISIONS UNLESS I INITIAL EITHER OR BOTH OF THE FOLLOWING BOXES:

IF I INITIAL THIS BOX [_____], MY HEALTH CARE SURROGATE'S AUTHORITY TO RECEIVE MY HEALTH INFORMATION **TAKES EFFECT IMMEDIATELY.**

IF I INITIAL THIS BOX [_____], MY HEALTH CARE SURROGATE'S AUTHORITY TO MAKE HEALTH CARE DECISIONS FOR ME TAKES EFFECT IMMEDIATELY. PURSUANT TO SECTION 765.204(3), FLORIDA STATUTES, ANY INSTRUCTIONS OR **HEALTH CARE DECISIONS I MAKE, EITHER VERBALLY OR IN WRITING, WHILE I POSSESS CAPACITY SHALL SUPERSEDE ANY INSTRUCTIONS OR HEALTH CARE DECISIONS MADE BY MY SURROGATE** THAT ARE IN MATERIAL CONFLICT WITH THOSE MADE BY ME.

Signature:_____ Date:_____

Address: _____

WITNESS #1

Signature:_____ Date:_____

Address: _____

WITNESS #2

Signature:_____ Date:_____

Address: _____

CHAPTER 12
FORM 6: LIVING WILL

IN FORM CAN REFUSE FURTHER MEDICAL CARE WHICH IS EXTREME ACTION

This form lets person do extreme act of blocking most health care if **later** doctors think person has irrevocable terminal condition and more care likely won't help. This form is more often used inside hospital or other facility since it's too long to read outside. This statutory form is found at Florida Statutes § 765.393. **This form is usually done only by sickest or oldest people.**

IN FORM CAN PICK HOW BAD MUST HEALTH BE BEFORE TREATMENT STOPS

In form person can pick how bad must health be before medical treatment stops, and options are either a) "terminal illness", b) "end-stage condition", or c) "persistent vegetative state". A person doing form can pick 1, 2, or 3 of the options, and many pick all 3. Of course, person if able to understand and communicate can directly refuse care by talking to doctors directly, so the form only matters if person is "incapacitated". The legislature has said giving food and water by tube or machine if person can't consume it themselves is included in what form may stop. A doctor usually explains form to patients and often provides copies to use. Basically, if a person's health gets so bad the form is triggered then pain relief and comfort care is still given but other treatment stops and the request in the form is followed that (as form says):

"life-prolonging procedures be withheld or withdrawn when the application of such procedures would serve only to prolong artificially the process of dying, and that I be permitted to die naturally with only the administration of medication or the performance of any medical procedure deemed necessary to provide me with comfort care or to alleviate pain."

MOST PEOPLE SKIP NAMING SURROGATE OR GIVING MORE INSTRUCTIONS

In form someone can be named "Surrogate" to help and push doctors to do as form says, but most people skip this since doctors and family usually will follow the form. And in form some instructions can be written but most people also skip this since it's hard to write clear instructions for all situations that won't risk delay or lawyers debating it. Hospitals and similar may have their own form they prefer. After doing form a person is usually free to override it, like by saying, "I want C.P.R. and all care, and cancel my Living Will."

FORM IS SIGNED BY DOCTOR OR SIMILAR AND THEN THE PATIENT

To be valid form must be signed by person doing form and 2 witnesses who must be at least age 18 and at least 1 can't be spouse of sick person or a blood relative of them. Once form is done a person should show it to doctors at all places it may be used to add it to medical files so it is followed. Usually a person keeps some copies in case needed. A person also usually shows form to family so they can explain it to any new doctors and health personnel.

LIVING WILL
(Florida Statutes § 765.303)

Declaration made this _____ day of _____, 20_____ , that I, _____ , willfully and voluntarily make known my desire that my dying not be artificially prolonged under the circumstances set forth below, and I do hereby declare that, if at any time I am incapacitated and

_____   I have a terminal condition, or
(initial)

_____   I have an end-stage condition, or
(initial)

_____   I am in a persistent vegetative state
(initial)

and if my primary physician and another consulting physician have determined that there is no reasonable medical probability of my recovery from such condition, I direct that life-prolonging procedures be withheld or withdrawn when the application of such procedures would serve only to prolong artificially the process of dying, and that I be permitted to die naturally with only the administration of medication or the performance of any medical procedure deemed necessary to provide me with comfort care or to alleviate pain.

It is my intention that this declaration be honored by my family and physician as the final expression of my legal right to refuse medical or surgical treatment and to accept the consequences for such refusal.

In the event that I have been determined to be unable to provide express and informed consent regarding the withholding, withdrawal, or continuation of life-prolonging procedures, I wish to designate, as my surrogate to carry out the provisions of this declaration:

Signature:_____   Phone:_____

Address:_____

I understand the full import of this declaration, and I am emotionally and mentally competent to make this declaration.

Additional Instructions (optional): _____

_____

_____

WITNESS #1
Signature:_____   Date:_____
Address: _____

WITNESS #2
Signature:_____   Date:_____
Address: _____

CHAPTER 13
FORM 7: DO NOT RESUSCITATE ORDER

IN FORMS CAN REFUSE HEALTH CARE WHICH IS EXTREME ACTION

There are really 2 forms in this chapter, and they let do extreme act of saying **starting immediately** to not provide some health care listed on form, like C.P.R. These form are more often used outside hospital or other medical facility since forms are short so paramedics can read them fast, but these forms also can be used inside places. **These forms are rarely used and usually only by sickest or oldest people.**

DO NOT RESUSCITATE ORDER FORM STOPS C.P.R. FROM BEING GIVEN

The Do Not Resuscitate Order form basically says C.P.R. should not be given which is cardio-pulmonary resuscitation to restart heart or breathing. This form is short 1 page so paramedics or similar people can read and follow it fast, and this form is mostly but not totally used by people outside hospital or similar place. Pain relief and comfort care is usually still given, so sick person is still usually taken to hospital even if form was done. A person can override form like by not showing form to paramedics or just telling them, "I now want C.P.R. and all care". A doctor usually explains the form and gives out copy to use on yellow paper.

P.O.L.S.T. FORM HAS OPTIONS TO REFUSE MORE KINDS OF HEALTH CARE

The P.O.L.S.T. form which stands for Physician Orders For Life Sustaining Treatment is like a Do Not Resuscitate Order form since it stops some health care, but the P.O.L.S.T. covers more kinds of treatment. People should read the form and discuss options with their doctor. The P.O.L.S.T form is longer with many paragraphs so though it technically can be used anywhere and paramedics or similar should try to follow it, the P.O.L.S.T. mainly is used inside a hospital or similar place where there is usually more time to read it.

FORMS ARE SIGNED BY PERSON AND THEIR DOCTOR

Forms in this Chapter to be completed must be signed by person and the person's doctor. Once a form is done people should show it at all places it may be used to add it to medical files so it can be followed. Usually a person also keeps copies to show paramedics, EMTs, or other people who want to give care. A copy of a form is often kept on bedside table, on home refrigerator (paramedics often look here), pinned to chest, in pocket, or some people wear a " bracelet" or similar made by companies chosen by the state. Usually a person also shows form to family so they explain to doctors, paramedics, and others if needed.

DO NOT RESUSCITATE ORDER
State of Florida, Section 401.45, Florida Statutes

Florida HEALTH

Patient's Full Legal Name: _____ Date of Birth: _____

(Print or Type)

PATIENT'S (OR AUTHORIZED PERSON'S) STATEMENT

Being informed of my right to refuse cardiopulmonary resuscitation (CPR), including artificial ventilation, cardiac compression, endotracheal intubation, and defibrillation, I direct that CPR be withheld or withdrawn from me.

By: _____ Date: _____

(Signature of Patient or Authorized Person)

I, _____, am authorized to sign on the patient's behalf as the patient's

(Print or Type Name of Authorized Person)

☐ principal, ☐ surrogate, ☐ proxy, or ☐ the minor patient's principal (per s. 765.101, F.S.); or I am expressly authorized to make the patient's health care decisions pursuant to a ☐ guardianship (per s. 744.102, F.S.), or ☐ power of attorney (per s. 709.08, F.S.).

HEALTH CARE PROVIDER'S STATEMENT

I, _____, provider license number _____,

(Print Full Legal Name)

am the patient's ☐ physician, ☐ osteopathic physician, ☐ autonomous advanced practice registered nurse, or ☐ physician assistant authorized by law to sign this order. I direct the withholding or withdrawal of CPR from the patient in the event of the patient's cardiac or respiratory arrest.

By: _____ Date: _____ Ph: _____

(Signature of Health Care Provider)   (Date Signed)   (Emergency)

A copy of this document printed on yellow paper (any shade) is valid as the original.

-- (Cut Along Line for Wallet Card) --

FLORIDA HEALTH **DO NOT RESUSCITATE ORDER**

State of Florida
Section 401.45, Florida Statutes

PATIENT'S OR AUTHORIZED PERSON'S STATEMENT

I, _____, being informed

(Print or Type Full Legal Name and Date of Birth)

of my right to refuse cardiopulmonary resuscitation (CPR), including artificial ventilation, cardiac compression, endotracheal intubation, and defibrillation, direct that CPR be withheld or withdrawn from me.

By: _____ Date: _____

(Signature of Patient or Authorized Person)   (Date Signed)

_____

(Print or Type Name of Authorized Person)

I am the patient's ☐ principal, ☐ surrogate, ☐ proxy, or ☐ the minor patient's principal (per s. 765.101, F.S.); or I am expressly authorized to make the patient's health care decisions pursuant to a ☐ guardianship (per s. 744.102, F.S.), or ☐ power of attorney (per s. 709.08, F.S.).

Fold Here

HEALTH CARE PROVIDER'S STATEMENT

I, _____,

(Print or Type Full Legal Name)

provider license number _____, am the patient's ☐ physician, ☐ osteopathic physician, ☐ autonomous advanced practice registered nurse, or ☐ physician assistant authorized by law to sign this order. I direct the withholding or withdrawal of CPR from the patient in the event of the patient's cardiac or respiratory arrest.

By: _____ Date: _____

(Signature of Health Care Provider)   (Date Signed)

Phone: _____

(Emergency)

Form DH 1896, Revised 06/2022, Incorporated by Rule 64J-2.018, F.A.C.

Physician Orders for Life-Sustaining Treatment (POLST)-Florida

Follow these orders until orders are reviewed. These medical orders are based on the patient's **current** medical condition and preferences. Any section not completed does not invalidate the form and implies full treatment for that section. With significant change of condition new orders may need to be written.

Patient Last Name	Patient First Name	Middle Int.

Date of Birth: (mm/dd/yyyy) ___ ___ ___ Gender ☐ M ☐ F Last 4 SSN: ☐ ☐ ☐ ☐

If the patient has decision-making capacity, the patient's presently expressed wishes should guide his or her treatment

A
Check One

CARDIOPULMONARY RESUSCITATION (CPR): Patient is unresponsive, pulseless, and not breathing.

☐ **Attempt Resuscitation/CPR**

☐ **Do Not Attempt Resuscitation/DNR**

When not in cardiopulmonary arrest, follow orders in B and C.

B
Check One

MEDICAL INTERVENTIONS: If patient has pulse and is breathing.

☐ **Full Treatment – goal is to prolong life by all medically effective means.**
In addition to care described in Comfort Measures Only and Limited Additional Interventions, use intubation, advanced airway interventions, and mechanical ventilation as indicated. Transfer to hospital and /or intensive care unit if indicated.
Care Plan: Full treatment including life support measures in the intensive care unit.

☐ **Limited Medical Interventions – goal is to treat medical conditions but avoid burdensome measures**
In addition to care described in Comfort Measures Only, use medical treatment, antibiotics, IV fluids and cardiac monitor as indicated. No intubation, advanced airway interventions, or mechanical ventilation. May consider less invasive airway support (e.g. CPAP, BiPAP). **Transfer to hospital if indicated. Generally avoid the intensive care unit.**
Care Plan: Provide basic medical treatments.

☐ **Comfort Measures Only (Allow Natural Death) – goal is to maximize comfort and avoid suffering**
Relieve pain and suffering through the use of any medication by any route, positioning, wound care and other measures. Use oxygen, suction and manual treatment of airway obstruction as needed for comfort. **Patient prefers no transfer to hospital for life-sustaining treatments. Transfer if comfort needs cannot be met in current location. Consider hospice or palliative care referral if appropriate.**
Care Plan: Maximize comfort through symptom management.

Additional Orders:_____

C
Check One

ARTIFICIALLY ADMINISTERED NUTRITION: Offer food by mouth if feasible.

☐ **Long-term artificial nutrition by tube.**   Additional Instructions:_____

☐ **Defined trial period of artificial nutrition by tube.**   _____

☐ **No artificial nutrition by tube.**   _____

D
Check One

HOSPICE or PALLIATIVE CARE (complete if applicable) - consider referral as appropriate

☐ Patient/Resident Currently enrolled in Hospice Care	☐ Patient/Resident Currently enrolled in Palliative Care	☐ Not indicated or refused
Contact:_____	Contact:_____	

SIGNATURES

Print Physician Name	MD/DO License #	Phone Number
Physician Signature **(mandatory)**	Date	
Print Patient/Resident or Surrogate/Proxy Name	Relationship (write 'self' if patient)	
Patient or Surrogate Signature **(mandatory)**	Date	

SEND FORM WITH PATIENT WHENEVER TRANFERRED OR DISCHARGED

Use of original form is strongly encouraged. Photocopies and facsimiles of completed POLST are legal and valid.

E Check All That Apply	DOCUMENTATION OF DISCUSSION:		
	☐ Patient (Patient has capacity)	☐ Health Care Representative or surrogate	
	☐ Parent of minor	☐ Court-Appointed Guardian	☐ Other (proxy)

Other Contact Information

Name of Guardian, Surrogate or other Contact Person	Relationship	Phone Number/Address	
Name of Health Care Professional Preparing Form	Preparer Title	Phone Number	Date Prepared

Directions for Health Care Professionals

Completing POLST

- Must be completed by a health care professional based on medical indications, a discussion of treatment benefits and burdens, and elicitation of patient preferences.

- POLST must be signed by a MD/DO to be valid. Verbal orders are acceptable with follow-up signature by physician in accordance with facility/community policy.

- POLST must be signed by patient/resident or healthcare surrogate/proxy to be valid.

Using POLST

- Any section of POLST not completed implies full treatment for that section.

- Use of original form is strongly encouraged. Photocopies and FAXes of signed POLST forms are legal and valid.

- A semi-automatic external defibrillator (AED) should not be used on a person who has chosen "Do Not Attempt Resuscitation."

- Oral fluids and nutrition must always be offered if medically feasible.

- When comfort cannot be achieved in the current setting, the person, including someone with "comfort measures only," should be transferred to a setting able to provide comfort, such as a hospice unit.

- A person who chooses either "comfort measures only" or "limited additional interventions" should not be entered into a Level I trauma system.

- An IV medication to enhance comfort may be appropriate for a person who has chosen "Comfort Measures Only."

- A person who desires IV fluids should indicate "Limited Interventions" or "Full Treatment."

- A person with capacity or the surrogate/proxy (if patient lacks capacity) can revoke the POLST at any time and request alternative treatment.

Reviewing POLST

This POLST should be reviewed periodically and a new POLST completed if necessary when:
(1) The person is transferred from one care setting or care level to another, or
(2) There is a substantial change in the person's health status, or
(3) The person's treatment preferences change.

To void this form, draw line through sections A through D on page 1 and write "VOID" in large letters.

Review of this POLST Form

Review Date	Reviewer	Location of Review	Review Outcome
			☐ No Change ☐ Form Voided ☐ New form completed
			☐ No Change ☐ Form Voided ☐ New form completed
			☐ No Change ☐ Form Voided ☐ New form completed

SEND FORM WITH PERSON WHENEVER TRANSFERRED OR DISCHARGED

REVISED FORM (JULY 10, 2015)

CHAPTER 14
FORM 8: DURABLE POWER OF ATTORNEY

FORM LETS POWER BE GIVEN OVER PROPERTY, MONEY, AND MORE

This form lets person give power to someone to let them do things with person's money, property, debt, and other things. Some people call this a "Financial Power Of Attorney". This form is called "durable" since it continues to have power even if person who did form is incapacitated, but power of the form ends at death.

FORM GIVES POWER TO LET SOMEONE HELP WITH PROPERTY AND MONEY

Form lets "Principal" give power to "Agent" or "Attorney-in-Fact" (both these terms are used) to do things involving Principal's money, property, and other things. Often Agent is trusted person like spouse or friend. The form lets Agent help do chores, pay bills, move money in accounts, buy or sell items, sign contracts, take out debt, and get information from others. This can help if person is sick, busy, or away, and may let person avoid nursing home, guardian, or conservator. A person till incapacitated can still overrule or fire Agent so really power is shared. In form powers given can be picked which can reduce risk of misuse, but if power is not clear banks and others may not obey Agent so most people give most or all possible powers. When Agent signs anything it should be like, "Ed Doe signing as Agent under Power of Attorney for Ann Po".

DUE TO RISKS INCLUDING FRAUD MANY SKIP FORM OR ASK LAWYER

Doing this form can be risky and lead to loss of money and property since an Agent can do dumb or criminal actions like stealing property, wasting money on dumb items, or just causing harm by carelessness. Agents have a "duty of care" and can be sued later but they might be out of money so can't undo their harm. Usually banks or others can't be blamed for obeying an Agent. Many people ask a lawyer for advice.

IT MAY BE IMPROPER FOR AGENT TO MAKE GIFTS OR DO OTHER THINGS

This area of law is complex and basic acts may be fine like paying bills, moving funds, or getting records. But less usual acts may be improper and even a crime by Agent like as gift handing out money or property to family or friends, making risky investments, or doing unusual acts. Many people ask a lawyer for advice.

SIGN FORM BEFORE NOTARY OR TWO WITNESSES

For form to be valid it should be signed by person doing it before a notary, and 2 witnesses must also sign after either seeing person doing the form sign or after they confirm and acknowledge it's their signature. Witnesses can't be named Agent or Attorney-in-Fact in the form. Once signed the form can be kept till needed or given quickly to Agent to hold. Some people show form quickly to banks or similar to get them to see it should be followed. Last page of form is done by Agent later if requested by a bank or other party. To cancel form a person should tell Agent and take back copies, and maybe tell all people who saw form.

DURABLE POWER OF ATTORNEY

This Power of Attorney is not affected by subsequent incapacity of the Principal except as provided in Florida Statutes § 709.08. This power of attorney is effective immediately and will continue until it is revoked.

I, _____, as Principal, hereby appoint _____ as my Attorney-in-Fact to act for me in any lawful way with respect to the following initialed subjects:

(Initial where Attorney-in-Fact shall have power and authority)

_____ 1. Personal Property. To do any action involving personal property including lease, sell, mortgage, purchase, exchange, and acquire, and to agree, bargain, and contract for the lease, sale, purchase, exchange, and acquisition of, and to accept, take, receive, and possess any personal property whatsoever, tangible or intangible, or interest thereto, on such terms and conditions, and under such covenants, as my Attorney-in-Fact shall deem proper; to have access to safe deposit boxes and remove all con- tents and relinquish or surrender the safe deposit box; and to maintain, repair, improve, manage, insure, rent, lease, sell, convey, subject to liens or mortgages, or to take any other security interests in said property which are recognized under the Uniform Commercial Code as adopted at that time under the laws of the State of Florida or any applicable state, or otherwise pledge and in any way or manner deal with all or any part of any real or personal property whatsoever, tangible or intangible, or any interest therein, that I own at the time of execution or may thereafter acquire, under such terms and conditions, and under such covenants, as my Attorney-in-Fact shall deem proper.

_____ 2. Real Property. To do any action involving real estate and fixtures including lease, sell, mortgage, purchase, exchange, and acquire, and to agree, bargain, and contract for the lease, sale, purchase, exchange, and acquisition of, and to accept, take, receive, and possess any interest in real property whatsoever, now owned or hereafter acquired, including my Homestead Property, on such terms and conditions, and under such covenants, as my Attorney-in-Fact shall deem proper; and to maintain, repair, tear down, alter, rebuild, improve, manage, insure, move, rent, lease, sell, convey, subject to liens, mortgages, and security deeds, and in any way or manner deal with all or any part of any interest in real property whatsoever, including specifically, but without limitation, real property lying and being situated in the State of Florida, under such terms and conditions, and under such covenants, as my Attorney-in-Fact shall deem proper and may for all deferred payments accept purchase money notes payable to me and secured by mortgages or deeds to secure debt, and may from time to time collect and cancel any of said notes, mortgages, security interests, or deeds to secure debt.

_____ 3. Transacting of Business. To conduct, engage in, and otherwise transact the affairs of any and all lawful business ventures of whatever nature or kind that I may now or hereafter be involved in. To organize or continue and conduct any business which term includes, without limitation, any farming, manufacturing, service, mining, retailing or other type of business

operation in any form, whether as a proprietorship, joint venture, partnership, corporation, trust or other legal entity; operate, buy, sell, expand, contract, terminate or liquidate any business; direct, control, supervise, manage or participate in the operation of any business and engage, compensate and discharge business managers, employees, agents, attorneys, accountants and consultants; and, in general, exercise all powers with respect to business interests and operations which the principal could if present and under no disability.

_____ 4. Banking Transactions. To conduct banking transactions as provided in Section 709.2208(1) of the Florida Statues, including all the actions mentioned in this Statute.

_____ 5. Investment Transactions. To conduct investment transactions as provided in Section 709.2208(2) of the Florida Statutes, including all the actions mentioned in this Statute.

_____ 6. Safe Deposit Boxes. To enter, access, remove items including money and documents, place items, open new boxes in my or other name, terminate any box and related lease, and to also do all these things with boxes held jointly with another or over any box I myself somehow have access or rights.

_____ 7. Claims, Litigation, and Settlement. To commence, prosecute, discontinue, or defend all actions or other legal proceedings touching my property, real or personal, or any part thereof, or touching any matter in which I or my property, real or personal, may be in any way concerned. To defend, settle, adjust, make allowances, compound, submit to arbitration or mediation, and compromise all accounts, reckonings, claims, and demands whatsoever that now are, or hereafter shall be, pending between me and any person, firm, corporation, or other legal entity, as my Attorney-in-Fact shall deem proper. To take legal action to enforce this document or concerning the Attorney-in-Fact's power to act for me.

_____ 8. Borrowing of Funds. To borrow for me and on my behalf any sum or sums of money on such terms and with such security as my Attorney-in-Fact may deem appropriate, and for that purpose to execute all promissory notes, bonds, mortgages and other instruments which may be necessary or proper.

_____ 9. Vehicles. To do any action involving any vehicle I now own or shall at any time hereafter acquire, including at any time to execute vehicle transfers, and also to buy, sell, lease, repair, store, or take other action with said vehicles.

_____ 10. Insurance Policies. To act as my attorney-in-fact or proxy in respect to any policy of insurance on my life or health, or any other type of insurance, and in such capacity to exercise any rights, privileges or options which I may have thereunder or pertaining thereto, and additional insurance of any type may be obtained as my attorney-in-fact deems proper. My Attorney-in-Fact will NOT under any circumstances have any power or incident of ownership whatsoever with respect to any life insurance policy owned by me under which my Attorney-in-Fact is the insured.

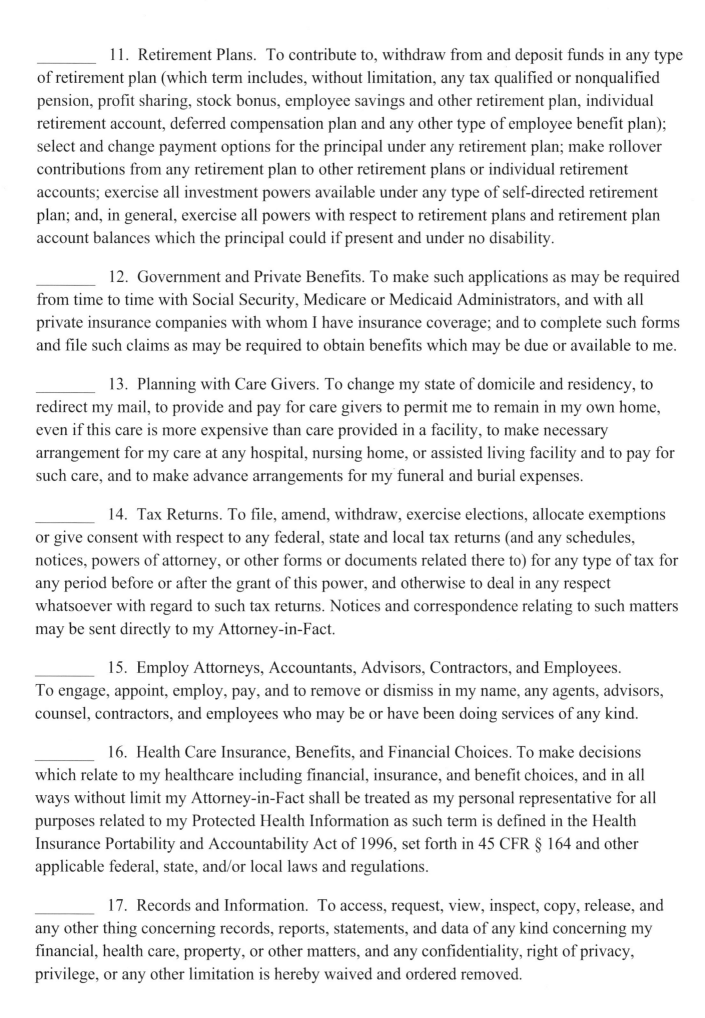

_____ 11. Retirement Plans. To contribute to, withdraw from and deposit funds in any type of retirement plan (which term includes, without limitation, any tax qualified or nonqualified pension, profit sharing, stock bonus, employee savings and other retirement plan, individual retirement account, deferred compensation plan and any other type of employee benefit plan); select and change payment options for the principal under any retirement plan; make rollover contributions from any retirement plan to other retirement plans or individual retirement accounts; exercise all investment powers available under any type of self-directed retirement plan; and, in general, exercise all powers with respect to retirement plans and retirement plan account balances which the principal could if present and under no disability.

_____ 12. Government and Private Benefits. To make such applications as may be required from time to time with Social Security, Medicare or Medicaid Administrators, and with all private insurance companies with whom I have insurance coverage; and to complete such forms and file such claims as may be required to obtain benefits which may be due or available to me.

_____ 13. Planning with Care Givers. To change my state of domicile and residency, to redirect my mail, to provide and pay for care givers to permit me to remain in my own home, even if this care is more expensive than care provided in a facility, to make necessary arrangement for my care at any hospital, nursing home, or assisted living facility and to pay for such care, and to make advance arrangements for my funeral and burial expenses.

_____ 14. Tax Returns. To file, amend, withdraw, exercise elections, allocate exemptions or give consent with respect to any federal, state and local tax returns (and any schedules, notices, powers of attorney, or other forms or documents related there to) for any type of tax for any period before or after the grant of this power, and otherwise to deal in any respect whatsoever with regard to such tax returns. Notices and correspondence relating to such matters may be sent directly to my Attorney-in-Fact.

_____ 15. Employ Attorneys, Accountants, Advisors, Contractors, and Employees. To engage, appoint, employ, pay, and to remove or dismiss in my name, any agents, advisors, counsel, contractors, and employees who may be or have been doing services of any kind.

_____ 16. Health Care Insurance, Benefits, and Financial Choices. To make decisions which relate to my healthcare including financial, insurance, and benefit choices, and in all ways without limit my Attorney-in-Fact shall be treated as my personal representative for all purposes related to my Protected Health Information as such term is defined in the Health Insurance Portability and Accountability Act of 1996, set forth in 45 CFR § 164 and other applicable federal, state, and/or local laws and regulations.

_____ 17. Records and Information. To access, request, view, inspect, copy, release, and any other thing concerning records, reports, statements, and data of any kind concerning my financial, health care, property, or other matters, and any confidentiality, right of privacy, privilege, or any other limitation is hereby waived and ordered removed.

Any Special Instructions: _____

_____

_____

_____

_____

_____

_____

_____

_____

_____

_____

_____

_____

_____

_____

_____

_____

_____

_____

     I hereby grant unto my Attorney-in-Fact named below full power and authority to execute all instruments, and to do everything appropriate and necessary to be done for me and in my name, as set forth herein.

     This instrument shall be governed by the laws of Florida, however it is my intention that it shall be valid and exercisable in any other state or jurisdiction including where I or my family have property.

     I agree any party or person who receives a copy of this document may act under it.

Revocation of the power of attorney is not effective as to a third party until they learn of the revocation.

I agree to indemnify the third party for any claims that arise against the third party because of reliance on this power of attorney.

SIGNATURE

Signed:_____   Date:_____

WITNESSES

On the date written above, the Principal declared to me in my presence that this document is his or her power of attorney and that he or she had willingly signed as his or her free and voluntary act for the purposes expressed.

Witness #1 Signature   Witness #2 Signature

_____   _____

Witness #1 printed name   Witness #2 printed name

_____   _____

NOTARY

Sworn to and subscribed before me on _____, 20___, by _____, who produced the following identification:_____.

_____ (Notary or official)

ACKNOWLEDGMENT OF AGENT (OPTIONAL)

BY ACCEPTING OR ACTING UNDER THE APPOINTMENT AND USING THAT POWER OF ATTORNEY DONE BY _____ AND DATED _____, THE AGENT AGREES THEY ASSUME THE FIDUCIARY AND OTHER LEGAL RESPONSIBILITIES OF AN AGENT.

Signature of Agent:_____ Date:_____

Printed Name of Agent:_____

- -

AFFIDAVIT OF AGENT / ATTORNEY IN FACT FOR SOME PARTY (OPTIONAL)

STATE OF FLORIDA   )
COUNTY OF _____) ss.

Before me, the undersigned authority, personally appeared _____
(attorney in fact), ("Affiant"), who swore or affirmed that:

1. Affiant is the attorney in fact named in the Florida General Durable Power of Attorney executed by _____ (principal) ("Principal") on _____ (date).

2. This Florida Durable Power of Attorney is currently exercisable by Affiant. The principal is domiciled in _____ (insert name of state or foreign country).

3. To the best of the Affiant's knowledge after diligent search and inquiry:
   a. The Principal is not deceased; and
   b. There has been no revocation, partial or complete termination by adjudication of incapacity or by the occurrence of an event referenced in the durable power of attorney, or suspension by initiation of proceedings to determine incapacity or to appoint a guardian.

4. Affiant agrees not to exercise any powers granted by the Florida Durable Power of Attorney if Affiant attains knowledge that it has been revoked, partially or completely terminated, suspended, or is no longer valid because of death or adjudication of incapacity of the Principal.

_____

[Signature of Affiant]

CERTIFICATE OF ACKNOWLEDGMENT OF NOTARY PUBLIC

Sworn to (or affirmed) and subscribed before me this ____ day of _____, 20____ by _____ [name of agent]. The affiant is [choose one:] ____ personally known to me, or ____ produced the following identification:_____

Signature of Notarial Officer:_____

My commission expires: _____

CHAPTER 15
FORM 9: DESIGNATION OF HEALTH CARE SURROGATE FOR MINOR

FORM LETS PARENT GIVE POWER TO SOMEONE OVER MINOR CHILD

This form lets parent or similar give someone power over health care decisions for minor child under 18.

FORM GIVES SOMEONE POWER OVER CHILD'S HEALTH CARE

Form lets parent give power over health care of child under 18 to someone named in the form called the "Surrogate" or less often "Agent". The parent keeps power and person given power in form can be overruled or fired anytime by the parent. This form can avoid delay if a medical problem with a child arises and medical people feel health care needs to be authorized quickly. Some people use this form often, like if child stays with relative a week, if child is at daycare daily, or if child is with coach or teacher for week. Note, some people do "Power Of Attorney Over Child", to give more power like school, discipline, and home, and this is a Power of Attorney form with most powers cut and words added giving Agent powers like, "all powers this parent has involving my child named _____ including health care, school, discipline, and home".

PEOPLE MUST SIGN FORM BEFORE NOTARY

For form to be valid parent signs in front of 2 witnesses who then sign too. Witnesses can be anyone at least 18 and not being given power in the form. Either 1 parent can sign alone or both 2 parents can sign which can make it likelier others people follow the form. A completed form can be kept till needed or immediately handed to person given power. Some people show form quickly to doctors, schools, and other places to get them to know it should be followed if ever needed. To cancel form a parent should tell person given power it is cancelled, take back copies, and tell anyone shown the form to not follow it.

DESIGNATION OF HEALTH CARE SURROGATE FOR MINOR
(Florida Statutes § 765.2035)

I/We,_____ , the
(check a box) [   ] natural guardian(s) as defined in s. 744.301(1), Florida Statutes;
            [   ] legal custodian(s);   [   ] legal guardian(s)
of the following minor(s):

_____ ,

_____ ,

_____ ,

pursuant to s. 765.2035, Florida Statutes, designate the following person to act as my/our surrogate for health care decisions for such minor(s) in the event that I/we am/are not able or reasonably available to provide consent for medical treatment and surgical and diagnostic procedures:

Name:_____
Address:_____
Phone:_____

If my/our designated health care surrogate for a minor is not willing, able, or reasonably available to perform his or her duties, I/we designate the following person as my/our alternate health care surrogate for a minor:

Name:_____
Address:_____
Phone:_____

I/We authorize and request all physicians, hospitals, or other providers of medical services to follow the instructions of my/our surrogate or alternate surrogate, as the case may be, at any time and under any circumstances whatsoever, with regard to medical treatment and surgical and diagnostic procedures for a minor, provided the medical care and treatment of any minor is on the advice of a licensed physician.

I/We fully understand that this designation will permit my/our designee to make health care decisions for a minor and to provide, withhold, or withdraw consent on my/our behalf, to apply for public benefits to defray the cost of health care, and to authorize the admission or transfer of a minor to or from a health care facility.

I/We will notify and send a copy of this document to the following person(s) other than my /our surrogate, so that they may know the identity of my/our surrogate.

SIGNATURE OF ONE OR TWO PARENTS OR SIMILAR:

Signature:_____ Date:_____

Signature:_____ Date:_____

TWO WITNESSES:
Signature:_____ Signature:_____

CHAPTER 16
FORM 10: INTER VIVOS AUTHORIZATION OF LEGALLY AUTHORIZED PERSON (FUNERAL AND REMAINS)

LETS PERSON BE NAMED TO CONTROL FUNERAL AND ANY CREMATION

This form lets person be named to control funeral, ceremonies, burial, and cremation. This can also be done in Will or Designation Of Health Care Surrogate. "Inter Vivos" in name of form means made during life.

IN FORM CAN NAME AGENT TO CONTROL FUNERAL AND RELATED MATTERS

In form a person can be named "Legally Authorized Person" to make decisions about funeral, burial, cremation, and related matters. Normally by law closest family control this starting with spouse, adult child, parents, and then siblings, but a small fraction of people don't want this like if family may be upset while mourning, bad with money, or do things person didn't want. The form has a spot to give instructions, and then spot to say any pre-arrangements already made like a pre-paid burial plot or burial insurance. Family and all other people legally must do what person wrote or clearly ever said was wanted if person left enough to afford it. Many people skip written instructions and trust people to act wisely or do what person said they wanted in private talks. Payment for funeral and similar comes from pre-paid funeral accounts, insurance, and estate or decedent's money and property, and Executor or family must help arrange payment.

SEVERAL OPTIONS EXIST FOR PEOPLE TO PICK

After a death police are told then <u>funeral home or crematorium comes get body</u>. About half of people pick burial and half cremation. With cremation, "cremains" go to family or "columbarium" vault in cemetery.

Half of people <u>do not do early events in first month</u> when shocked family may be unready for visitors. Importantly, if "Direct Burial" or "Direct Cremation" is requested quickly costs may be 80% off usual $10,000+ but this skips events with body till well after burial or cremation (close family maybe can see burial from afar). Months later these people often do "Celebration", "Remembrance", or "Ash Scattering" at house, park, church, rented hall, or funeral home, often with food, speech, or video, but maybe no remains present to be less sad.

Half of people <u>do early events in first month</u>, and there are several complicated options to pick from. <u>First</u>, some people do within days a "Vigil", "Viewing", or "Wake", where family and friends talk or pray maybe in room with body (with closed or open casket) or cremated ashes, often done at Funeral Home or church. <u>Second</u>, some people do big ceremony within week of either a) funeral (maybe with Mass) in church with priest or minister, or b) informal event like "Celebration of Life" or "Remembrance" with or without body. <u>Third</u>, some people do final event at cemetery, religious or not, like a burial or putting ashes in a vault. Note, if event uses body not just ashes it usually is at funeral home, church, or cemetery and within weeks.

SIGN FORM WITH 2 WITNESSES

The form must be signed before a notary by person doing form and 2 witnesses who then sign too. A form should be kept so it's found quickly within days of death, or it can be handed out to someone to hold. The form can be canceled like by throwing it away or telling other people it is cancelled.

Inter Vivos Authorization and Direction of Legally Authorized Person
(Funeral And Remains)

I, _____ (print name), called "Declarant" in this document, being of sound mind, do hereby make the following designation and choices:

1. I designate _____ to be my "Legally authorized person" under the provisions of Florida Statutes § 497.005 (43) to make funeral arrangements and Florida Statutes § 497.607 to dispose of my remains including by cremation. Legally authorized person now named should follow first the intentions expressed in this document and second any pre-arrangements that I have made at an earlier time.

2. For my funeral, cremation, and/or disposition of body I hereby say I choose the following: _____

_____

_____

_____

_____

_____

_____

_____

_____.

3. If pre-arrangements have been made for my funeral, cremation, and/or disposition of my body they are as follows including payment arrangements:

_____

_____.

4. Legally authorized person named above shall not be entitled to a fee for acting in such capacity but shall be entitled to be reimbursed for out of pocket expenses, such as travel fees and attorney's fees in defending his or her actions, to be paid by the personal representative of my estate without order of Court.

5. I intend my funeral arrangements, any disposition of my cremated remains, and related matters to be governed by Florida laws existing when I sign this document.

Date:_____ Signature of Declarant:_____

Witness:_____ Witness:_____

NOTARY

STATE OF FLORIDA   )
) ss.
COUNTY OF _____)

I, _____, say and declare to the officer taking my acknowledgment of this instrument, and to the signing witnesses, that I signed this instrument as my Inter Vivos Declaration.

Signature of Declarant:_____

We, _____ and _____, have been sworn by the officer signing below, and declare to that officer on our oaths that the Declarant declared the instrument to be her Inter Vivos Declaration and signed it in our presence, and that we each signed the instrument as a witness in the presence of the Declarant and of each other.

Signature of witness:_____

Signature of witness:_____

Acknowledged and signed before me by Declarant, _____, who is personally known to me or sufficiently proven, and sworn to and signed before me by witnesses, _____ and _____, both of whom are personally known to me or sufficiently proven, and signed by me in the presence of Declarant and witnesses, all on the ___ of _____, 20__.

Notary Public, State of Florida:_____

APPENDIX:
HOW TO GET FORMS AND
SOME SAMPLE FILLED-OUT FORMS

TO GET FORMS TO USE PEOPLE CAN:

(1) PHOTOCOPY BOOK PAGES,

(2) TEAR OUT PAGES FROM A BOOK, OR

(3) DOWNLOAD BOOK WITH FORMS FROM WWW.DAVENPORTPUBLISHING.COM.

EMAIL ANY COMMENTS TO DAVENPORTPRESS@GMAIL.COM.

On the next pages to show how it can be done are some sample fill-in legal forms.

All forms can be filled out by pen, marker, or pencil (and most people do this), and using a computer or typewriter to neatly complete forms is not legally required.

All signatures and dates by signatures should be handwritten with permanent pen or marker and not done by a computer or typewriter.

Anyone can filled in a form, like friend with neat writing can fill in all parts of a Will or other form, and only final signatures and nearby date or address must be done by each person signing.

For forms with blank spaces to add words to people can add words in many ways. Some people use a pen or marker or even pencil, some use computer but are not too neat, and some use a computer to add a word and then delete all left-over lines.

Any of these is fine:

"I appoint ___*John Doe*___ as Agent" ,

"I appoint ___John Doe___ as Agent",

"I appoint John Doe as Agent".

People need not worry about neatness or small mistake, and a document is usually fine if those people who knew a decedent in life can tell the likely meaning.

When doing forms it may help to know "respectively" means "in order just stated".

LAST WILL AND TESTAMENT

I, ___*Susan Lee Maxwell*___, of ___*Duval*___ County, Florida, do revoke all prior Wills, Testaments, and Codicils, and do make, publish, and declare this as my Will. When doing this I am of sound mind and under no duress or undue influence.

1. GIFTS. I give these gifts but to get a gift the recipient must survive the Testator, except as otherwise stated below.

I give _____ SKIPPED _____ to _____.

I give _____ to _____.

I give _____ to _____.

I give _____ to _____.

I give _____ to _____.

I give _____ to _____.

I give _____ to _____.

I give _____ to _____.

I give _____ to _____.

I give _____ to _____.

I give _____ to _____.

2. GIFTS OF TANGIBLE PERSONAL PROPERTY BY SEPARATE WRITINGS. I may give tangible personal property by writings separate from a Will as allowed by state law, but writings not found within 90 days of my death shall be canceled and of no effect.

3. RESIDUE. I give the rest and residue and remainder of my estate, my property of any kind and nature, and anything I have an interest in (all of which is called the "residue"), so long as any such thing was not transferred by other Will provisions, as follows:

   a) to _Paul Thomas Maxwell_ who survive me with persons just named who survive me taking the share of non-survivors, then

   b) to _Jennifer Pamela Maxwell and Oscar Kent_ and if any of those just named do not survive me their part goes to their lineal descendants, per stirpes.

4. ADMINISTRATION. I name and appoint _Paul Thomas Maxwell_ as Personal Representative including for me, my Will, and my estate.

5. MISCELLANEOUS. The following applies to this Will and generally.

Priority of Will gifts of the same type is based on the order they are written.

The words "give" and "gift" also means a devise, bequest, grant, legacy, or similar.

If gift or gift section mentions survival, survive, or surviving then survival is an absolute condition and anti-lapse laws or similar have no effect.

In this document no unfilled part is a mistake and residue spaces may be left blank.

Any failure to make gifts to family including children is intentional and not a mistake.

No gift or transfer made during life reduces or offsets a Will gift unless during my life I expressly called it a "loan" or "advancement".

Use of particular gender shall include other genders, reference to singular or plural shall be interchangeable, and "they" may be singular or plural.

If context permits the terms Personal Representative, Executor, and Administrator shall be seen as interchangeable as if all were written, and if context permits Guardian of the Property is interchangeable with Guardian of the Estate and Conservator.

Any Personal Representative may anytime pay or settle claims or debts they in their sole discretion find proper or helpful to pay, but I specifically say any secured debts including mortgages or liens on real property or vehicles should not be paid off unless parts of this Will specify it.

I give any person named or acting as Personal Representative the fullest power and discretion allowed by state law, and I grant them all powers that may be conferred on Personal Representatives by state law.

Any Personal Representative shall not be required to render and file annual accountings with respect to property or money including in relation to my Will or estate.

I authorize informal probate of my estate and Will and also administrative probate if any Personal Representative chooses, and any Personal Representative may act

independently in all ways without supervision including from any court or judge.

I give any Personal Representative authority to lease, sell, mortgage, convey, or retain property of mine in such manner and time they deem in the best interest, helpful, or proper.

The residue includes lapsed or failed gifts, insurance paid to estate, inheritances owed me, and property I had a power of appointment or testamentary disposition over.

If in Florida or other place a Conservator, Administrator, Guardian of the Property, or any other fiduciary is needed for a child of mine or their estate or property, or for any other person, then I appoint for that the person named Personal Representative above.

Any Personal Representative, Guardian, Executor, Conservator, or fiduciary under this Will or otherwise, shall qualify and serve without bond, surety, security, or similar, including despite their place of residence or lack of relationship to any state or country.

TESTATOR

IN WITNESS WHEREOF, I, _Susan Lee Maxwell_ , sign, publish, and declare this instrument as my Will, this __22nd__ day of __June__ , 20 _22_ .

Susan Lee Maxwell
Testator signature

WITNESSES

The foregoing instrument was signed by the Testator and Testator declared it to be the Testator's Will, which signing and declaration was made in the presence of us the witnesses, and we do now sign our names in this document below as witnesses at the request and in the presence of the Testator and presence of each other on this _22nd_ day of _June_ , 20 _22_ .

Nancy Ann Smith
Witness #1 signature

24 Main St., Bond, FL 33882
Witness #1 address

Pamela Bonnie Rooker
Witness #2 signature

15 Roy St., Bond, FL 33881
Witness #2 address

LAST WILL AND TESTAMENT

I, <u>Henry James Ford</u>, of <u>Miami-Dade</u> County, Florida, do revoke all prior Wills, Testaments, and Codicils, and do make, publish, and declare this to be my Will. When doing this I am of sound mind and under no duress or undue influence.

1. GIFTS. I give these gifts but to get a gift the recipient must survive the Testator, except as otherwise stated below.

I give <u>big oak table</u> to <u>Anne J. Wix.</u>

I give <u>$5,000</u> to <u>Loretta Marsha Switt in the hope she will help her young daughter Megan Kara Switt</u>.

I give <u>63 Ivy Road, Lundy, Florida, 34087</u> to <u>Greta Olivia Fox.</u>

I give <u>all land in Troy, Florida</u> to <u>Greta Olivia Fox.</u>

I give <u>9087 Wilderness Road, Bozeman, MT</u> to <u>James Tiberius Smith.</u>

I give <u>Bronze Roman Lamp</u> to <u>Anne Kilby</u> and <u>Kevin Kilby.</u>

I give <u>wedding ring</u> to <u>Ruth Jones.</u>

I give <u>all jewelry not given above</u> to <u>Kay Pidoski.</u>

I give <u>$7,281.35</u> to <u>Wanda Kay Zinski</u>.

I give <u>UBank account #8980443723</u> to <u>Joy Rundy a friend</u>.

I give <u>1998 Ford truck</u> to <u>John Smith my uncle.</u>

I give <u>a total of $50,000</u> to <u>Brian Peterson, Michael Peterson, and Mary Hart</u>.

I give <u>Wells Fargo acct ending in #8923</u> to <u>Lawrence Deer</u>.

I give <u>$1,000</u> to <u>that charity food kitchen on Smith Avenue in Kilby, Florida.</u>

I give <u>all extra spare tires I own at my death</u> to <u>Victor Perez my mechanic</u>.

I give <u>$6,000 in total</u> to <u>my cousin Carol Brown's children</u>.

I give <u>$500 each</u> to <u>each of my grandchildren</u>.

2. GIFTS OF TANGIBLE PERSONAL PROPERTY BY SEPARATE WRITINGS.

I may give tangible personal property by writings separate from a Will as allowed by state law, but writings not found within 90 days of my death shall be canceled and of no effect.

3. RESIDUE.
I give the rest and residue and remainder of my estate, my property of any kind and nature, and anything I have an interest in (all of which is called the "residue"), so long as any such thing was not transferred by other Will provisions, as follows:

   a) to _____ Pamela Bonnie Ford my wife _____ who survive me with persons just named who survive me taking the share of non-survivors, then

   b) to my kids Ron Ford, Kevin Ford, Tina Ford, and Vera Hill and if any of those just named do not survive me their part goes to their lineal descendants, per stirpes.

4. ADMINISTRATION.
I name and appoint   Pamela Bonnie Ford my wife   as Personal Representative including for me, my Will, and my estate.

5. MISCELLANEOUS.
The following applies to this Will and generally.

Priority of Will gifts of the same type is based on the order they are written.

The words "give" and "gift" also means a devise, bequest, grant, legacy, or similar.

If gift or gift section mentions survival, survive, or surviving then survival is an absolute condition and anti-lapse laws or similar have no effect.

In this document no unfilled part is a mistake and residue spaces may be left blank.

Any failure to make gifts to family including children is intentional and not a mistake.

No gift or transfer made during life reduces or offsets a Will gift unless during my life I expressly called it a "loan" or "advancement".

Use of particular gender shall include other genders, reference to singular or plural shall be interchangeable, and "they" may be singular or plural.

If context permits the terms Personal Representative, Executor, and Administrator shall be seen as interchangeable as if all were written, and if context permits Guardian of the Property is interchangeable with Guardian of the Estate and Conservator.

Any Personal Representative may anytime pay or settle claims or debts they in their sole discretion find proper or helpful to pay, but I specifically say any secured debts including mortgages or liens on real property or vehicles should not be paid off unless parts of this Will specify it.

I give any person named or acting as Personal Representative the fullest power and discretion allowed by state law, and I grant them all powers that may be conferred on Personal Representatives by state law.

Any Personal Representative shall not be required to render and file annual accountings with respect to property or money including in relation to my Will or estate.

I authorize informal probate of my estate and Will and also administrative probate if any Personal Representative chooses, and any Personal Representative may act independently in all ways without supervision including from any court or judge.

I give any Personal Representative authority to lease, sell, mortgage, convey, or retain property of mine in such manner and time they deem in the best interest, helpful, or proper.

The residue includes lapsed or failed gifts, insurance paid to estate, inheritances owed me, and property I had a power of appointment or testamentary disposition over.

If in Florida or other place a Conservator, Administrator, Guardian of the Property, or any other fiduciary is needed for a child of mine or their estate or property, or for any other person, then I appoint for that the person named Personal Representative above.

Any Personal Representative, Guardian, Executor, Conservator, or fiduciary under this Will or otherwise, shall qualify and serve without bond, surety, security, or similar, including despite their place of residence or lack of relationship to any state or country.

TESTATOR

IN WITNESS WHEREOF, I, *Henry James Ford* sign, publish, and declare this instrument as my Will, this *30th* day of *December,* 20*27.*

Henry James Ford
Testator signature

WITNESSES

The foregoing instrument was signed by the Testator and Testator declared it to be the Testator's Will, which signing and declaration was made in the presence of us the witnesses, and we do now sign our names in this document below as witnesses at the request and in the presence of the Testator and presence of each other on this *30th* day of *December*, 20*27.*

Olivia Joy Pawlenty	87 Hastings Avenue, Buffalo, FL 33450
Witness #1	Address #1
Roy Felix Pawlenty	87 Hastings Avenue, Buffalo, FL 33450
Witness #2	Address #2

LAST WILL AND TESTAMENT

I, ___Ruth May Kent___ , of __Broward__ County, Florida, do revoke all prior Wills, Testaments, and Codicils, and do make, publish, and declare this to be my Will. When doing this I am of sound mind and under no duress or undue influence.

1. GIFTS. I give these gifts but to get a gift the recipient must survive the Testator, except as otherwise stated below.

I give silverware and copper bathtub and Jetski to Ann Porter my niece.

I give 1987 Ford Truck and any other vehicles I own to Bill Porter my nephew.

I give $2,000 to Greg Best but if he fails to survive then his wife Jo Best.

I give $1,000 to the American Red Cross charity.

I give $2,250 to St. Joseph's my church.

I give $300 to Timmy Hart my paperboy.

I give a total of $10,000 50% to Abraham Daniel Walker, 40% to Amy Ann Hope, and 10% to Jennifer Kim Beaufort.

I give $1,300 and my cat Garfield to Sara Ham who I trust to care for him.

I give $5,000 to Juanita Chuzappa my Home Nurse but if she fails to survive me then to her children.

I give $100 to each of my first cousins.

I give $7,002.21 to Brenda Hill but if she fails to survive her son Eric Hill.

2. GIFTS OF TANGIBLE PERSONAL PROPERTY BY SEPARATE WRITINGS.
I may give tangible personal property by writings separate from a Will as allowed by state law, but writings not found within 90 days of my death shall be canceled and of no effect.

3. RESIDUE. I give the rest and residue and remainder of my estate, my property of any kind and nature, and anything I have an interest in (all of which is called the "residue"), so long as any such thing was not transferred by other Will provisions, as follows:

   a) to <u>Ken Rufus Kent my husband</u> who survive me with persons just named who survive me taking the share of non-survivors, then

   b) to <u>my young children Pamela Sue Kent and Adam David Kent</u> and if any of those just named do not survive me their part goes to their lineal descendants, per stirpes.

4. ADMINISTRATION. I name and appoint <u>Ken Rufus Kent my husband</u> as Personal Representative including for me, my Will, and my estate.

5. GUARDIANS. I name and nominate <u>Helen Olivia Kent my sister</u> as Guardian of the Person of any child of mine or other person without full legal capacity. I name and nominate <u>Ken Rufus Kent my husband</u> as Guardian of the Property of any minor child or infant of mine or other person without full legal capacity, and this person I name should be guardian for their money, property, and estate.

6. MISCELLANEOUS. The following applies to this Will and generally.

   Priority of Will gifts of the same type is based on the order they are written.

   The words "give" and "gift" also means a devise, bequest, grant, legacy, or similar.

   If gift or gift section mentions survival, survive, or surviving then survival is an absolute condition and anti-lapse laws or similar have no effect.

   In this document no unfilled part is a mistake and residue spaces may be left blank.

   Any failure to make gifts to family including children is intentional and not a mistake.

   No gift or transfer made during life reduces or offsets a Will gift unless during my life I expressly called it a "loan" or "advancement".

   Use of particular gender shall include other genders, reference to singular or plural shall be interchangeable, and "they" may be singular or plural.

   If context permits the terms Personal Representative, Executor, and Administrator shall be seen as interchangeable as if all were written, and if context permits Guardian of the Property is interchangeable with Guardian of the Estate and Conservator.

   Any Personal Representative may anytime pay or settle claims or debts they in their sole discretion find proper or helpful to pay, but I specifically say any secured debts including mortgages or liens on real property or vehicles should not be paid off unless parts of this Will specify it.

   I give any person named or acting as Personal Representative the fullest power and

discretion allowed by state law, and I grant them all powers that may be conferred on Personal Representatives by state law.

Any Personal Representative shall not be required to render and file annual accountings with respect to property or money including in relation to my Will or estate.

I authorize informal probate of my estate and Will and also administrative probate if any Personal Representative chooses, and any Personal Representative may act independently in all ways without supervision including from any court or judge.

I give any Personal Representative authority to lease, sell, mortgage, convey, or retain property of mine in such manner and time they deem in the best interest, helpful, or proper.

The residue includes lapsed or failed gifts, insurance paid to estate, inheritances owed me, and property I had a power of appointment or testamentary disposition over.

If in Florida or other place a Conservator, Administrator, Guardian of the Property, or any other fiduciary is needed for a child of mine or their estate or property, or for any other person, then I appoint for that the person named Personal Representative above.

Any Personal Representative, Guardian, Executor, Conservator, or fiduciary under this Will or otherwise, shall qualify and serve without bond, surety, security, or similar, including despite their place of residence or lack of relationship to any state or country.

TESTATOR

IN WITNESS WHEREOF, I, _Ruth May Kent_   did sign, publish, and declare this instrument as my Will, this 22nd day of July, 2021.

Ruth May Kent
Testator signature

WITNESSES

The foregoing instrument was signed by the Testator and Testator declared it to be the Testator's Will, which signing and declaration was made in the presence of us the witnesses, and we do now sign our names in this document below as witnesses at the request and in the presence of the Testator and presence of each other on this 22nd day of July, 2021.

Susan Harriet Rogers   87 Badger Road, Jacksonville, FL, 33307
Witness #1   Address #1

Lucy Ann Pamway   892 Franklin Street, Atlanta, GA 30301
Witness #2   Address #2

LAST WILL AND TESTAMENT

I, **David Eric Smith**, a resident of **Pinellas** County, Florida do revoke all prior Wills, Testaments, and Codicils, and do make, publish, and declare this to be my Will. When doing this I am of sound mind and under no duress or undue influence.

1. GIFTS. I give these gifts but to get a gift the recipient must survive the Testator, except as otherwise stated below.

I give _____ to _____.

I give _____ to _____.

I give _____ to _____.

I give _____ to _____.

I give _____ to _____.

I give _____ to _____.

I give _____ to _____.

I give _____ to _____.

I give _____ to _____.

2. GIFTS OF TANGIBLE PERSONAL PROPERTY BY SEPARATE WRITINGS.
I may give tangible personal property by writings separate from a Will as allowed by state law, but writings not found within 90 days of my death shall be canceled and of no effect.

3. RESIDUE. The rest and residue and remainder of my estate, my property of any kind and nature, and anything I have an interest in, I give to **Nancy Ann Smith and Pamela Bonnie Rooker my daughters who survive me**, and to lineal descendants per stirpes of a person just named who did not survive me.

4. ADMINISTRATION. I name and appoint **Nancy Ann Smith** my daughter as as Personal Representative including for me, my Will, and my estate.

5. MISCELLANEOUS. The following applies to this Will and generally.

Priority of Will gifts of the same type is based on the order they are written.

The words "give" and "gift" also means a devise, bequest, grant, legacy, or similar.

If gift or gift section mentions survival, survive, or surviving then survival is an absolute condition and anti-lapse laws or similar have no effect.

In this document no unfilled part is a mistake and residue spaces may be left blank.

Any failure to make gifts to family including children is intentional and not a mistake.

No gift or transfer made during life reduces or offsets a Will gift unless during my life I expressly called it a "loan" or "advancement".

Use of particular gender shall include other genders, reference to singular or plural shall be interchangeable, and "they" may be singular or plural.

If context permits the terms Personal Representative, Executor, and Administrator shall be seen as interchangeable as if all were written, and if context permits Guardian of the Property is interchangeable with Guardian of the Estate and Conservator.

Any Personal Representative may anytime pay or settle claims or debts they in their sole discretion find proper or helpful to pay, but I specifically say any secured debts including mortgages or liens on real property or vehicles should not be paid off unless parts of this Will specify it.

I give any person named or acting as Personal Representative the fullest power and discretion allowed by state law, and I grant them all powers that may be conferred on Personal Representatives by state law.

Any Personal Representative shall not be required to render and file annual accountings with respect to property or money including in relation to my Will or estate.

I authorize informal probate of my estate and Will and also administrative probate if any Personal Representative chooses, and any Personal Representative may act independently in all ways without supervision including from any court or judge.

I give any Personal Representative authority to lease, sell, mortgage, convey, or retain property of mine in such manner and time they deem in the best interest, helpful, or proper.

The residue includes lapsed or failed gifts, insurance paid to estate, inheritances owed me, and property I had a power of appointment or testamentary disposition over.

If in Florida or other place a Conservator, Administrator, Guardian of the Property, or any other fiduciary is needed for a child of mine or their estate or property, or for any other person, then I appoint for that the person named Personal Representative above.

Any Personal Representative, Guardian, Executor, Conservator, or fiduciary under this Will or otherwise, shall qualify and serve without bond, surety, security, or similar, including despite their place of residence or lack of relationship to any state or country.

TESTATOR

IN WITNESS WHEREOF, I, _David Eric Smith_ , sign, publish, and declare this instrument as my Will, this _21st_ day of _____ _June_ , 20 _21_.

David Eric Smith
Testator signature

WITNESSES

The foregoing instrument was signed by the Testator and Testator declared it to be the Testator's Will, which signing and declaration was made in the presence of us the witnesses, and we do now sign our names in this document below as witnesses at the request and in the presence of the Testator and presence of each other on this _21st_ day of _June_ , 20 _21_.

Nancy Ann Smith   204 Main Street, Buffalo, FL 33987
Witness signature   Witness address

Pamela Bonnie Rooker   83 River Road, Lakeville, FL 33428
Witness signature   Witness address

64

SELF-PROVING AFFIDAVIT

(Florida Statutes § 732.503)

STATE OF FLORIDA

COUNTY OF _PINELLAS_

I, _David Eric Smith_ , Testator, declare to the officer taking my acknowledgment of this instrument, and to the subscribing witnesses, that I signed this instrument as my Will.

David Eric Smith
Testator

We, _Nancy Ann Smith_ and _Pamela Bonnie Rooker_ have been sworn by the officer signing below, and declare to that officer on our oaths that the Testator declared the instrument to be the testator's Will and signed it in our presence and that we each signed the instrument as a witness in the presence of the Testator and of each other.

Nancy Ann Smith
Witness

Pamela Bonnie Rooker
Witness

ACKNOWLEDGED AND SUBSCRIBED before me by means of physical presence of the Testator, _David Eric Smith_ , who is (check a box) [**X**] personally known to me or [ ] has produced identification in the form of _____ , and

sworn to and subscribed before me by both physically present two witnesses: _Nancy Ann Smith_ who is (check a box) [**X**] personally known to me or [ ] has produced identification in the form of _____ , and _Pamela Bonnie Rooker_ who is (check a box) [**X**] personally known to me or [ ] has produced identification in the form of _____ .

Subscribed by me in the presence of the Testator and the subscribing witnesses, by the means specified herein, all on the _21st_ day of _June_ , 20 _21_ .

JOHN M. SMITH
MY COMMISSION #DD050500
EXPIRES: JUNE 27, 2027

John M. Smith
Notary Public: State of Florida

65

TANGIBLE PERSONAL PROPERTY LIST

My Will may refer to separate writings making gifts to occur at death and I do this writing for that purpose including as allowed by Florida Statutes § 732.515.

I understand in this writing only tangible personal property can be given and also only things not specifically disposed of by Will.

I may do many pages of these writings at different times and they all should be seen as 1 document, and if any conflicts occur the more recently done page controls.

If a person getting a gift below does not survive me such gift shall lapse and instead that property passes as my Will says including by a Will residue clause.

This page if not found within 90 days of my death shall have no effect.

PROPERTY ITEMS		NAMES OF RECIPIENTS
1998 Ford Truck	to	Samantha Bell
1.3 carat diamond ring + Irish rings	to	Ann Sue Reed
14 ft power boat + kayak + paddles	to	L. Wheeler
Parkhurst style bench	to	Reba Stewart
glass table, telescope, all umbrellas	to	Rebecca Stewart
18 wood cups, oak platter, oak vase	to	Mary and Cindy Lott
my wedding dress and shoes	to	Mary Lott
chainsaw with serial no. 382937	to	Mary Lott
chainsaw with serial no. 89930	to	Matt Smith
antique lanterns + repair kits	to	Sue Wu maid at Hart Hotel
oak lamp kept on porch	to	Mary Kay Poppler
sewing machines	to	Mary Kay Poppler
rocking chair bought in Oregon	to	Don Winkler boat mechanic
all fishing poles and fishing nets	to	Joe "Fish" Hoss, fishing pal
purple couch	to	Ken Baker
	to	

DATE: _12-12-2022_   SIGNED: _David Eric Smith_

Made in the USA
Columbia, SC
09 April 2023

14588173R00078